WRITING HISTORY

WRITING HISTORY

A Guide for Students

William Kelleher Storey

Millsaps College

FIFTH EDITION

New York   Oxford

OXFORD UNIVERSITY PRESS

Oxford University Press is a department of the University of Oxford.
It furthers the University's objective of excellence in research,
scholarship, and education by publishing worldwide.

Oxford   New York
Auckland   Cape Town   Dar es Salaam   Hong Kong   Karachi
Kuala Lumpur   Madrid   Melbourne   Mexico City   Nairobi
New Delhi   Shanghai   Taipei   Toronto

With offices in
Argentina   Austria   Brazil   Chile   Czech Republic   France   Greece
Guatemala   Hungary   Italy   Japan   Poland   Portugal   Singapore
South Korea   Switzerland   Thailand   Turkey   Ukraine   Vietnam

For titles covered by Section 112 of the US Higher Education
Opportunity Act, please visit www.oup.com/us/he for the
latest information about pricing and alternate formats.

Published by Oxford University Press
198 Madison Avenue, New York, NY 10016
http://www.oup.com

Oxford is a registered trademark of Oxford University Press.

Library of Congress Cataloging-in-Publication Data
Storey, William Kelleher.
   Writing history : a guide for students / William Kelleher Storey
(Millsaps College). -- Fifth edition.
      pages cm
   Includes bibliographical references and index.
   ISBN 978-0-19-023894-0 (paperback : acid-free paper)
 1. History--Research. 2. Academic writing. 3. Historiography. I. Title.
   D16.S864 2016
   907.2--dc23

                                                2014042377

Printing number: 9 8 7 6 5 4 3

Printed in the United States of America
on acid-free paper

CONTENTS

Contents

Contents

PREFACE

This book introduces the challenges of writing history. It contains technical advice, but it is more than just a style manual; it shows how historians select topics, analyze sources, and build arguments. In short, it is a practical guide for beginning historians.

Writing History had its origins in the Harvard Writing Project, a collaborative effort between Harvard's Expository Writing Program and other departments to improve undergraduate writing. Between 1995 and 1997, while I was teaching writing courses at Harvard, my chair, Nancy Sommers, put me in contact with professors from the History Department and the History of Science Department who were reforming the ways in which their departments taught writing. As I worked with faculty members, especially with Mark Kishlansky and Mark Madison, it became clear that both students and teachers would benefit from a short guide. I wrote two booklets for Harvard, and as I circulated drafts to friends and colleagues at other universities, I began to realize that there was a wide demand for a guide to writing history.

While working on the first edition, published in 1999, I benefited from the advice, comments, and criticism of Tony English, Jim Goodman, Gordon Harvey, Maura Henry, Bill Kirby, Mark Kishlansky, Susan Lively, Mark Madison, Everett Mendelsohn, Nancy Sommers, Mary Terrall, and Jon Zimmerman. Since that time, I have been teaching with the book at Millsaps College, where my students and colleagues have made a number of suggestions for improvement.

The second edition, published in 2004, incorporated important revisions, including expanded sections on plagiarism, interviewing, topic selection, and the use of the Internet in historical research. In preparing the second edition, I was helped by several anonymous reviewers, as well as Jan Beatty, Christine Lutz, Ellen Stroud, and, once again, Mark Kishlansky.

Over the years, it became clear that the second edition did not go far enough in embracing the Internet as a tool for historical research. In the third edition, published in 2009, I added more material on how to conduct research on the Internet. I also rearranged the first chapter, "Getting Started," to take into account how history students begin their research projects online. I made other changes, too, including recommendations for history students on how to become better peer editors. The book was reformatted as well, to make it easier to use as a reference. I received excellent advice about making these changes from five anonymous reviewers and also from my editor, Brian Wheel.

Only a few years later, developments on the Internet pushed me and my editors, Charles Cavaliere and Lynn Luecken, to make further improvements. While preparing a fourth edition and a fifth edition, I received helpful reviews from two dozen anonymous history professors, plus Charles Cavaliere, Andrew Paxman, and Drew Swanson. The third edition took a fairly open-ended approach to research on the Internet. The fourth and fifth editions still give general guidance for Internet searching, but they also take advantage of the existence of the Oxford Bibliographies Online, which provide knowledgeable, up-to-date guidance for students who are beginning research on unfamiliar topics. The fifth edition introduces new kinds of online research, ranging from sources to digital tools. Both the fourth and fifth editions also include a more accessible format.

One thing has not changed since the first edition. I still wish to acknowledge the six people who have done the most to encourage me to learn how to write history. They are my teachers, Philip Curtin, Robin Kilson, and Scotty Royce; my parents, Bill and Mary Storey; and my wife, Joanna Miller Storey.

Reviewers of the Fifth Edition

Manu Bhagavan, Hunter College-CUNY
Esperanza Brizuela-Garcia, Montclair State University
Trevor A. Corless, Heritage College
Alex Sayf Cummings, Georgia State University
R. Blake Dunnavent, Louisiana State University in Shreveport
Justin Horton, Thomas Nelson Community College
Annamarie Vallis, California State University, Fresno
David Van Heemst, Olivet Nazarene University
Kenneth Wilburn, East Carolina University
Allan M. Winkler, Miami University of Ohio

Introduction

Writing history is about making decisions. Historians choose from a broad range of subjects, selecting those they think are most important. They choose source materials carefully, assessing evidence that may support or contradict their arguments. And they choose ways to write, balancing respect for their subjects with the needs of their audience.

The best historians make choices so well that they can transform painstaking research into seamless arguments and narratives. Don't be fooled. On the surface history may seem straightforward, but the process of writing is filled with difficult decisions. As Peter Novick says in *That Noble Dream*, writing history, even with the best sources and methods, can be like trying "to nail jelly to a wall."[1] For this reason, historians experiment with many approaches to the past. Still, in the end they must choose an approach that suits their subject.

Ever since the days of the ancient Greeks, the process of selection has guided Western historical writing. Around 404 BCE, when the Athenian general Thucydides composed his history of the Peloponnesian Wars, he could not write about everything that had occurred in the thirty years of battles and defeats. Instead, he wrote an account that emphasized decisive moments, such as Pericles' famous eulogy for the Athenian dead. According to Thucydides, Pericles said:

> I have no wish to make a long speech on subjects familiar to
> you all: so I shall say nothing about the warlike deeds by which

> we acquired our power or the battles in which we or our fathers
> gallantly resisted our enemies, Greek or foreign. What I want
> to do is, in the first place, to discuss the spirit in which we
> faced our trials and also our constitution and the way of life
> which has made us great. After that I shall speak in praise of
> the dead. . . .[2]

Thucydides did not just include Pericles' eulogy because it was moving; he recounted the speech because he found it instructive.

Like Thucydides, modern-day historians also choose topics that shed light on contemporary problems. In 2000, John McNeill, a history professor at Georgetown University, published a book called *Something New Under the Sun: An Environmental History of the Twentieth-Century World*, in which he argued that twentieth-century people had achieved something unprecedented: human production and consumption had made global, negative impacts on the Earth's air, soil, and water. These patterns of destructive behavior were not sustainable, necessitating adaptation or decline. The implications for global politics were clear, particularly in light of ongoing discussions about climate change: if people would modify their behavior, then the survival of our species would be more likely.[3]

Like McNeill and Thucydides, historians choose subjects that they find important, and they explore these important subjects to seek the causes of change over time. To do this, historians choose from many possible methods. Enter the stacks of a library and browse through any shelf of history books. Notice that historians who work in narrow geographical and chronological specialties approach their subjects from a variety of perspectives. When historians write, they incorporate methods and insights from the work of other historians as well as from scholarship in the humanities, the natural sciences, and the social sciences. For example, in *The Columbian Exchange* Alfred Crosby depended on agronomy, anthropology, and epidemiology to explain early contacts between Aztecs and Spanish conquistadors.[4] Historians choose from so many approaches that it is difficult to place historical writing in facile categories.

Despite the diversity in historical writing, most historians share a commitment to good writing. Historians learn how to find sources and they know how to report on sources faithfully. Using their sources, they make inferences about the events of the past, and then they develop their inferences into sustained arguments and narratives. These must, in turn, be shaped by the conventions for writing good sentences and choosing appropriate words. Historians aspire to communicate their ideas about the past. They try to do so accurately and honestly.

1 Getting Started

There are many reasons to write history. Historians may be interested in explaining a particular source, in which case they must assess its significance in light of other sources. Perhaps they begin with an analytical problem that they have noticed in some body of historical literature, and they must seek out sources as a way of exploring the problem. Or, more prosaically, an instructor may assign them to write about a particular source or analytical problem; in this case the choices are limited. In any case, the only way to write history is to engage with source materials and other writers. This is challenging because it is not always a simple matter to find suitable sources and to engage the right writers. A full, careful review of the largest possible number of sources will help historical writers express ideas confidently.

There are several types of essays that history instructors commonly assign to their students. These are the book review, the analytical essay, and the research essay. Sometimes the research essay is limited to the course subject. In other cases, such as an honors thesis, the subject of the paper can be open-ended. The details of the assignment may vary, which means that students will need to pay careful attention to their professor's prompts. Writing about history is about analysis, not just collecting facts.

This chapter provides guidance for students who are writing research essays. Students who are writing shorter analytical essays, book reviews, and comparative essays can refer to the box titled "The Short Analytical Essay" in this chapter.

THE SHORT ANALYTICAL ESSAY

There are many types of analytical essays. Some analyze one source; others analyze two or more. Some analyze sources from the time period that is under study; others analyze works of history that have been written recently. A professor's prompt for the essay may instruct students to "assess," "compare," or "evaluate." All these requests are specific types of analysis. What does this word mean?

Analysis comes from the Greek word for "breaking apart." By breaking apart a historical source into its components, we are able to arrive at a greater understanding of it.

- Before composing the essay, the first step of analysis is to *describe*, in detail, the source. Who wrote it? What does it say? How is it written?
- The next step is to *compare* it with other sources from the time or about the time. Is it similar to, or different from, the other texts that describe these same things?
- The final step is to *argue* about the source. Put simply, an argument is a claim that can be argued about. What can you say about the source that can be argued about, on the basis of a reasonable consideration of the evidence?

The length and structure of an analytical essay will be determined by the professor. Typically such an essay begins with a paragraph that introduces the topic and states the main argument (or thesis) of the essay. Subsequent paragraphs are connected by "signpost" sentences, general sentences that make a connection from one paragraph to another. Chapter 5, "Get Writing! Get Organized," provides detailed instructions and examples that work just as well for a short analytical essay as they do for a long research essay.

The Book Review

The book review is one of the most common forms of analytical essay. A prompt might look something like this:

> In a three-to-five-page essay, write a review of William Cronon's book *Changes in the Land: Indians, Colonists, and the Ecology of New England* (New York: Hill and Wang, 1983, 2nd ed. 2003).

Historians read and discuss books all the time. In this case, imagine that students in a course about early U.S. history are reading William Cronon's

1

famous study of New England ecology. This is the book that introduced the importance of the environment to many historians. Reviewing a book such as this (after discussing it in class) should be a relatively straightforward matter.

Book reviews are anything but straightforward. Professors assign them because, in the words of historian Bruce Mazlish, "A book reviews the reviewer as much as the reviewer reviews the book."[1] The review will show how well—and how much—the reviewer reads.

The reviewer's first task is to identify the book's argument and to summarize it in his or her own words: "Cronon argues that British colonists in North America had an expansive view of capitalism, which led them to lay waste to much of the environment" (pp. vii–viii). That's the easy part. The next task is to place Cronon's argument into context. Does it resemble the arguments of other historians? Before Cronon wrote his book, some historians had already written about how Native Americans and settlers variously practiced subsistence and trade. After *Changes in the Land*, many historians followed him. What were the unique features of Cronon's argument?

The next step is to review how well the argument is supported by evidence. Cronon mined memoirs and journals from colonial America, plus latter-day scientific and historical analyses of New England's natural history. In a book review, it is important to highlight the evidence that is most—and least—persuasive. The book reviewer evaluates how well the evidence supports the argument. Reviewers may mention evidence that the author neglected, but out of fairness reviewers must refrain from criticizing an author for not writing the book that the reviewers would have written themselves!

The Comparative Essay

Prompt: in a three-to-five-page essay, analyze the famous 1855 speech of Chief Seattle, "How Can One Sell the Air," in light of what you have learned about U.S. environmental history from *Changes in the Land*.

In this case, we have two sources. The source by Chief Seattle is a primary source; in other words, it comes from the time period that we are studying. Cronon's book is a secondary work; it reflects back on another time and tries to understand it. (For more discussion about the differences between primary sources and secondary works, see pp. 32–33.)

The speech by Chief Seattle has found its way into many textbooks, collections, and websites. Typically these sources give some context: that the chief, for whom the city of Seattle is named, spoke these words to protest the incursions of settlers.

> How can one buy or sell the air, the warmth of the land?
> That is difficult for us to imagine.
> If we don't own the sweet air and bubbling water, how can you buy it from us?
> . . . So when the Great Chief in Washington sends word that he wants to buy our land, he asks a great deal of us.
> The earth is not his brother but his enemy and when he has conquered it he moves on.
> He cares nothing for the land, he forgets his father's grave and his children's heritage. . . .

In our notes, the first step is to describe the words of Chief Seattle and also to describe the ideas of William Cronon in *Changes in the Land* (this last part we have already done, earlier). Look for patterns in what they are saying. With a complete description, it seems apparent that Chief Seattle defends Native American environmental practices in the face of pressure from European settlers, the history of which Cronon has documented in his book. Both Seattle and Cronon contrast Native American and European American environmental practices, yet there are notable differences between their two contexts. Cronon's sources were from colonial New England; Chief Seattle lived in the Pacific Northwest during the first half of the nineteenth century. One possible argument could be made about the similarities: Cronon's arguments could be applied to other parts of the United States at other times.

This would be a superficial analysis. If your professor allowed you to use only these sources, this would be a reasonable conclusion. Even so, a bit of research into Chief Seattle's speech would reveal an interesting pattern. One historian, Albert Furtwangler, has written a book about the speech, *Answering Chief Seattle* (Seattle: University of Washington Press, 1997). Furtwangler reveals that the original text has never been found. Chief Seattle did speak at several meetings between chiefs and officials, although at the time the speeches were translated from Seattle's language, Duwamish, into a more common Native American language, Chinook, before being translated a third time into English. Errors in translation may have been compounded by the passage of time. It took more than thirty years before the first written account appeared, and it was written by an Anglo American who might not have even been there!

Source problems may generate interesting arguments. The chief's speech may be false, but his experiences were typical of Native American chiefs in the earliest decades of relations with Anglo-American settlers.

We may infer this from our knowledge of the evidence from Cronon. An- other possibility is that settler sources—including the author of the Seattle speech and the authors of many of Cronon's documents—may be suspect. Did settlers report what they *thought* about Native Americans without checking for the truth? Did Anglo-American settlers feel guilt about their environmental practices, and ascribe the opposite practices to the Native Americans, making them out to be nobler? Either way, the process of describing, comparing, and arguing can further our understanding of people in the past.

The rest of this book is concerned mainly with research essays. Even so, the chapters that follow contain advice for students who are working on shorter analytical essays, too. See especially Chapter 4, "Use Sources to Make Inferences"; Chapter 5, "Get Writing! Get Organized"; Chapter 7, "Writing Sentences in History"; Chapter 8, "Choose Precise Words"; and Chapter 9, "Revising and Editing."

1A Explore Your Interests

People are probably asking you about your interests all the time. At a party, you might find that the best approach is to condense your inter- ests into a crisp one-liner. When you write history, you will grapple with topics and questions that cannot be summarized so neatly. Writing projects present opportunities to clarify and develop your interests.

Historians become interested in research topics for all sorts of reasons. The history of medicine may interest you because you want to become a doctor; the history of physics may interest you because you are concerned about nuclear proliferation. Perhaps some histori- ans have inspired your interests, through either their teaching or their writing. Or an instructor may be requiring you to write about a specific topic. When you work on any writing project, use your sources to address questions that are significant to you.

1B Find a Historical Motive

An instructor has asked you to research and write a historical essay. The Internet makes possible a quick search on a search engine like

Google, followed by a link to Wikipedia. This may seem like a good beginning to many people, but to historians this is merely the opening serve in a long tennis match. Good writing starts with extensive and methodical reading. The more books, articles, and sources we read, the more authoritatively we may write. And writing requires active reading, which involves taking notes, tracking down references, and observing contradictions between authors. These contradictions are especially important. While you are reading, look for a motive, a contradiction that merits investigation. Two historians writing about the same topic rarely come to the same interpretation. Why are their views conflicting? Did they consider different evidence? Do they have opposing political commitments? Is there a way for you to test their arguments on another set of data and come to a conclusion of your own? Maybe all historians writing about a topic agree about some things, but your personal knowledge of the subject causes you to doubt their findings. Can you support your conflicting view with evidence?

1C Focus Your Interests Early

As you begin to read and write about a topic, recognize that you cannot adequately address a very broad topic in a relatively short essay. Even an essay that is twenty-five pages in length cannot cover, say, the history of the United States during the Second World War. Such topics usually are best approached by scholars who have more experience and time than do students. If you sense that your interests already are too broad, try the following exercise, which will help you to narrow down your topic.

If you are writing a guided research essay in a class about the Second World War, or if you are exploring a topic on the war for an open-ended research project, fill in the blanks in this sentence: "I am writing about the role of [blank] in [blank] during the Second World War." One possible answer might be "I am writing about the role of Japanese-American soldiers in Italy during the Second World War." Another answer could be "I am writing about the role of women in U.S. aircraft factories during the Second World War." The variations on the exercise are endless. They can help to bring some topical and geographical specificity to the beginning rounds of historical research.

1D Work with Bibliographies

There is so much history to write about, and so little time for writing. Deadlines put pressure on everyone, but it is possible to use this pressure to your advantage. The first thing to do is to convert your historical interests into a feasible research topic. Find a small story within your broad range of interests, and select only the best sources, especially if you have a strict page limit.

In a guided research essay, say, for a class about U.S. history, or in an open-ended research paper such as an honors thesis, it will be important to think about what you enjoy learning. Let us say that you have been fascinated by colonial America ever since a childhood visit to Colonial Williamsburg. Let us also say that like many citizens you are concerned about cross-cultural relations and the environment. You have read Cronon's *Changes in the Land*. You are inspired to write an environmental history of colonial America.

Unfortunately, this is the sort of topic that is best suited to a lengthy book and not a short essay. Chances are that you have limits to your time and number of pages. How can you find a topic that will help you explore your interests but also accommodate your limitations? The environmental history of colonial America is clearly a broad topic. Cronon's classic work addressed only colonial New England, and it took him years of research and more than two hundred pages of text to address it properly. If you are committed to writing about environmental history in colonial America, the topic may be narrowed down by asking, "Which geographical part of America?" You may wish to write about the town, state, or region where you live. Let us say you live in the Southeastern United States and are broadly familiar with the history of the region. And you share Cronon's interest in relations between colonists and Native Americans. Now the topic is narrowing. The resources available on the Internet and in the library can help you narrow your topic.

Most students begin a research project by searching the Internet, yet there is so much out there, and it is often difficult to determine which sources are reliable. Good guidance can be found in bibliographies, lists of readings that scholars assemble for fellow researchers. Often good bibliographies can be found at the end of works of history, as with Cronon's *Changes in the Land*, although in this case his bibliography focuses on colonial New England. How can you find a bibliography that focuses on the Southeast?

Ask a librarian. Librarians will probably not know about narrowly specialized knowledge, but they will know how to find a general bibliography about a subject. In your case, a librarian will probably search the library's catalog, or a database called WorldCat, which pulls together all library catalogs. A keyword search that combines "American environmental history" with the words "bibliography," "companion," and "handbook" reveals a number of promising sources, among them a book called *A Companion to American Environmental History*, edited by Douglas Cazaux Sackman. Go find the book in the reference room or in the stacks. It turns out to be rather thick, but a quick glance at the table of contents reveals there is one chapter, called "Cultures of Nature to ca. 1810," written by Matthew Dennis, that looks especially promising. Dennis has written an essay that surveys colonial U.S. environmental history, while the bibliography contains many works that address the Southeast.

It would be perfectly appropriate for you to start tracking down those books and skimming them in order to narrow your topic even further. It may also be more practical—and more enjoyable—simply to ask your professor. Chances are your professor will be happy to discuss a research topic, especially if you have a working bibliography and are developing specific ideas about your interests. Professors will be familiar with key works by other scholars and will be able to suggest books that provide helpful overviews and contain useful bibliographies. In the case of the environmental history of the Southeastern United States in the colonial period, the first book many professors will recommend is one that also appears in Dennis's bibliography, Timothy Silver's *A New Face in the Countryside: Indians, Colonists, and Slaves in South Atlantic Forests, 1500–1800.*

1D

As you begin to read Silver's book, you notice that it is comprehensive and accessible, much like Cronon's book. A careful review of the text and references reveals that Silver cites Cronon's book as an inspiration. Read Silver's book with an eye to narrowing your topic. What specific issues capture your attention? What passages do you, in turn, find inspiring? On page 43, Silver writes about Native American beliefs and rituals concerning plants and animals. After describing how Cherokee hunters practiced rituals to defend themselves against animal spirits, Silver turns to a description of ceremonies related to planting maize, or corn.

> Other rituals surrounded the plant world. Perhaps the most significant of these was the Green Corn Ceremony, an elaborate ritual of purification and celebration associated with the ripening of maize. Although the exact nature of the ceremony differed from group to group, the festival generally involved dancing, fasting, cleaning of houses and gathering places, building new fires, and forgiving transgressions of the previous year—all as part of an effort to thank the providers of the corn and start the new year with a clean body and spirit. William Bartram, a Quaker naturalist who traveled in the South during the mid-1770s, also discovered something of the Indian reverence for corn when a Cherokee chieftain offered him some for his horse. Bartram interpreted this gesture as an indication of "the highest esteem" since Indians believed "corn was given by the Great Spirit only for food for man." Wild plants inspired similar admiration. When gathering ginseng, an aromatic medicinal herb, the Cherokees spoke of it as a "sentient being . . . able to make itself invisible to those unworthy to gather it." In searching for the fragrant roots, Indian collectors passed over the first three plants they encountered and took the fourth only after offering a prayer and the gift of a small bead as compensation to the plant's spirit. After this gesture, other plants could be taken at will.

In writing this paragraph, Silver cites two modern works about Cherokee ceremonies as well as an original source from the eighteenth century, *Travels of William Bartram*. Bartram traveled in the South and wrote about Native Americans, so his book seems promising, given your interests. The next step is to search for Bartram's book, as well as other books, by following the clues in bibliographies and looking up works in WorldCat or in the library's online catalog.

The next step is to search for the most promising source, or sources, in WorldCat.

Good guidance can also be found in the Oxford Bibliographies Online. This resource is available through most college libraries. It is also available by personal subscription.

Go to the main page, www.oxfordbibliographiesonline.com (see Figure 1.1). For a project on cross-cultural relations and colonial American environmental history, click the box labeled "Atlantic History." (Atlantic History usually refers to the history of African, American, and European interactions from the late fifteenth century, when Columbus sailed from Spain to the Caribbean, to the late nineteenth century, when slavery ended in the Americas.)

Clicking "Atlantic History" opens a table of contents. Each title represents a specialized area of Atlantic History.

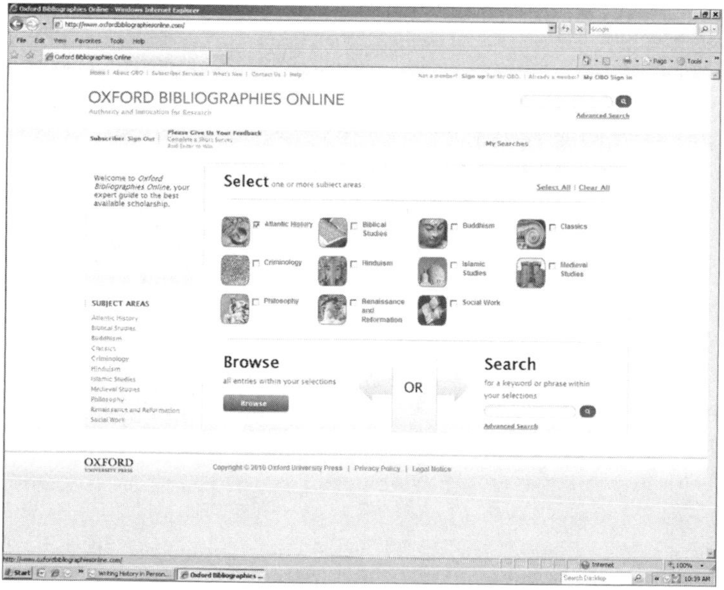

Figure 1.1

1D

Browse down and click "Environment and the Natural World." This opens a short essay by an expert scholar, Susan Scott Parrish, about Atlantic environmental history. Her essay will guide you through the next stages of research. For ease of reference, on the left a table of contents allows readers to navigate back and forth easily. The essay itself also contains links to sources and related essays. The essay may be printed or emailed.

Reading through the essay, you come upon some suggested sources from the colonial period, including William Bartram's *Travels,* which Parrish suggests contain accounts of Native Americans. To find the book, click the link to WorldCat. This is the same book referenced earlier, in the print bibliography by Silver.

WorldCat is part of the online reference collection of most college libraries. Click it and it will tell you whether or not your own library has a copy.

First WorldCat gives you a choice of editions (see Figure 1.2). In this case, you look for the exact title Parrish recommends. Choose one that looks up-to-date, the first one.

Figure 1.2

If I were doing this search myself, I would click on the WorldCat listing for Bartram's *Travels*. WorldCat determines my location and then lists a book in the library of Millsaps College, where I teach, while also suggesting that I look in the collections of several other libraries nearby. WorldCat links directly to my own college library's online catalog, where I can find the call number of the book and find the physical copy. In case I want to read an electronic copy, the library also links me to an edition of Bartram's *Travels* on Google Books (see Figure 1.3). The edition on Google Books dates to 1792, when the book was reprinted in London, after its 1791 publication in Philadelphia (see Figure 1.4). In those days, book titles were much more descriptive than they are today. You see from the title page that this work will discuss Bartram's travels among the Southeastern Native Americans. Bartram indicates right up front that he will review the region's natural environment, too. It is time to read! If you find it difficult to read on Google Books, WorldCat indicates several more recent print editions, too.

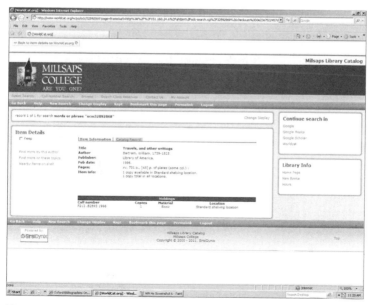

Figure 1.3

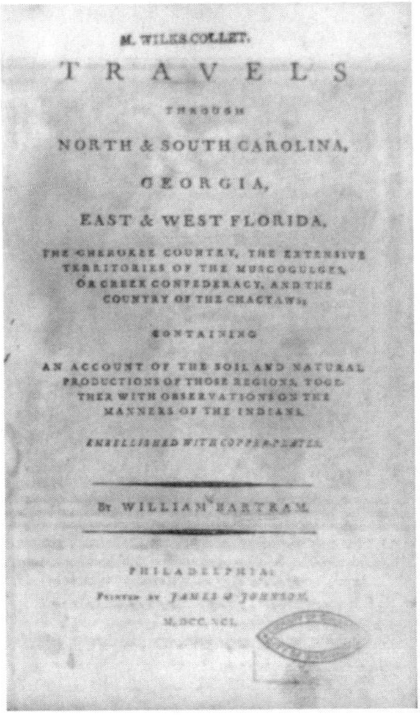
M. WILKS COLLET.

TRAVELS

THROUGH

NORTH & SOUTH CAROLINA,

GEORGIA,

EAST & WEST FLORIDA,

THE CHEROKEE COUNTRY, THE EXTENSIVE TERRITORIES OF THE MUSCOGULGES, OR CREEK CONFEDERACY, AND THE COUNTRY OF THE CHACTAWS;

CONTAINING

AN ACCOUNT OF THE SOIL AND NATURAL PRODUCTIONS OF THOSE REGIONS, TOGETHER WITH OBSERVATIONS ON THE MANNERS OF THE INDIANS.

EMBELLISHED WITH COPPER-PLATES.

BY WILLIAM BARTRAM.

PHILADELPHIA:

PRINTED BY JAMES & JOHNSON,

M,DCC,XCI.

Figure 1.4

1E Search Preselected Databases on the Internet

Thus far we have used print bibliographies as well as the Oxford Bibliographies Online to identify a broad range of sources for a research essay on colonial U.S. environmental history. Our search turned up many items.

The sheer amount of information available can be overwhelming. Thankfully, scholars, librarians, and archivists have selected specific collections of information that are worthy of consideration by scholars and that may be accessed online. Some of these sources are available free to everybody. Some of them require payment or subscription, whether by an individual or a library.

1. Search for Books in Online Library Catalogs. Most library catalogs are now digitized. Many are available online. The best way to search them is to use WorldCat, a digital library catalog that links library catalogs around the world. This is a widely used subscription service whose search results will indicate if your own library owns the book you are looking for. If it does not, a click of the mouse will take you to a page where you can order the book through Interlibrary Loan. If your local library does not subscribe to WorldCat, search the library's catalog first, and then turn to a large online catalog, such as the U.S. Library of Congress at http://catalog.loc.gov, where you may identify most of the books available on any particular subject. The key to searching a digital catalog is understanding how the information is organized. Most items in the library have an author, a title, or a subject heading. To find the right headings, start with a keyword search. In a keyword search, it is important to use distinctive words. Type in *environmental history* and you will get too many entries. A more specific search, like *colonial environmental*, will still produce too many entries. A narrower set of entries will be revealed if you follow the subject headings of any book that interests you. Click the subject headings to link to other works on the same subject. Note that subject searches differ from keyword searches. Keyword searches may turn up your word or words in widely varying order. By contrast, subject headings are fixed by the Library of Congress. You will get a hit on a subject heading only if you click on or type in its exact wording. (Just ask a librarian. All librarians will be able to explain to you how to search for Library of Congress subject headings.) Once you come across a useful subject heading, follow links to other subjects. Click on author and title links to help identify related works. For example, the subject headings for Bartram's *Travels* reveal much about the author and his adventures. WorldCat reveals a number of useful subject headings, including "Indians of North America—Southern States—Early Works to 1800." A click on that link reveals more travel narratives from the same time, including ones written by Bossu and Milfort. In addition, the subject heading search reveals a modern book about Bartram, *William Bartram on the Southeastern Indians*, by Gregory Waselkov and Kathryn Braund (Lincoln: University of Nebraska Press, 1995). These books, in turn, can be looked up simply by clicking them. If your own library does not own them, one more click on the button Get This Item from Another Library will place an order through Interlibrary Loan.

2. Search Journals in Online Databases. Articles and reviews from scholarly journals can often provide helpful guideposts to a field. Many libraries now subscribe to databases that allow users to search online indexes, such as Academic Search Premier offered by EBSCO Host. Sometimes these services grant users access to full-text versions of articles. When articles are not available through the databases, EBSCO Host gives citations that allow users to find hard-copy versions of the articles or to order them through Interlibrary Loan. Full-text versions of journal articles are available through JSTOR, Project Muse, and the History Cooperative. Together these provide subscribing libraries with access to recent issues and back issues of hundreds of journals.

3. Google Books. Google has embarked on an effort to digitize many of the world's books. They are doing so with the cooperation of some of the world's most important libraries. Google is making available the entire texts of books that were published before 1922, because they are no longer subject to copyright. Books that were published after 1922 may be purchased through Google or through other vendors. Go to http://books.google.com and search for *William Bartram*. This search yields many results.

4. Search Historical Websites. Sixteen years ago, the first edition of this book disparaged the Internet, saying it was filled with garbage and advising students to stay away from it. Today there are thousands of excellent Internet sites for scholars interested in history. Archives have placed documents and images online, as have newspapers and institutions. Many scholars have assembled websites that are informative and interactive.

- The Library of Congress has created the massive American Memory Project, http://memory.loc.gov, which provides online access to hundreds of thousands of documents, images, and recordings.
- The Library of Congress also coordinated the transfer of U.S. newspapers to a searchable, online database called Chronicling America, found at http://chroniclingamerica.loc.gov.

- The Digital Public Library of America, http://dp.la, is making thousands of items available online.
- The Center for History and New Media at http://chnm.gmu.edu at George Mason University contains traditional scholarship and source materials as well as access to digital media.
- National and local archives in many countries are making parts of their collections available online.
- There are also websites devoted to specific historical topics. The Slave Trade Database found at http://slavevoyages.org from Emory University covers the subject comprehensively.
- The Valley of the Shadow at http://valley.vcdh.virginia.edu allows scholars to explore in detail the history of two Civil War communities, one in Pennsylvania and the other in Virginia.
- The Victorian Web at http://www.victorianweb.org contains hundreds of articles and documents pertaining to all aspects of life in Victorian Britain.
- The Old Bailey Online, http://www.oldbaileyonline.org, contains the record of 197,745 criminal trials in Britain's most famous court from 1674 to 1913.
- One of the most extensive lists can be found at the Library of Congress "Virtual Reference Shelf," www.loc.gov/rr/askalib/virtualref.html

Sites like these—and many more—are making it possible for scholars to study about subjects that once required expensive research trips to distant locations. Now much of the work can be done at home; yet it can still be difficult to find good historical websites. Many college libraries now list websites that have become favored resources for historical researchers.

1F Use Reference Sources to Begin a Project

Fundamental reference works, including encyclopedias, dictionaries, and textbooks, survey a broad range of interests and topics. Most of these references are accessible over the Internet.

1. Encyclopedias. A strong encyclopedia can help you get an early, broad understanding of a topic. It will contain basic explanations as well as hints about related subjects. Just keep in mind that encyclopedias can provide only an introduction. If you write a paper based on encyclopedia articles, you will not impress your readers.

Nevertheless, the *Encyclopedia Britannica* does contain baseline information about the colonial United States, as well as illustrations and a bibliography. In this instance, an encyclopedia article could help to jump-start a research project. Search the online *Encyclopedia Britannica* for "United States history." A link appears to an article, "United States: History," that gives a broad overview. For a more advanced student of history, a search of "William Bartram" might be more helpful, in that the result reveals a short biography. It is also worth searching more specifically historical encyclopedias, which may be available online or in bound copies in the library reference section.

2. Dictionaries. Dictionaries are also a quick way to explore some topics. Be aware that there are three types of dictionary, each with its own special uses. *Prescriptive* dictionaries like *Webster's* tell you how words should be used; *descriptive* dictionaries like *American Heritage* tell you how words are actually used; and *historical* dictionaries like the *Oxford English Dictionary* tell you how words have been used over time.

In the case of colonial U.S. environmental history, dictionaries probably have little to offer, but they are still worth a look because you never know what you might find. Since you are considering Bartram's *Travels*, it might be interesting to check the word "naturalist" in the *Oxford English Dictionary*, since this is a word people used in describing Bartram in his own time. The *OED* suggests that the principal meaning of the word—"an expert in or a student of natural science; a natural philosopher; a scientist"—has not changed much since that time, although today a writer like Bartram might be more likely called a scientist or a nature writer. Other specialized dictionaries are commonly held in library reference and may prove useful, too. For example, the *Dictionary of American Biography* has an entry for Bartram. Even so, in this case the dictionary does not raise any interesting research questions.

3. Textbooks. Increasingly, history textbooks are available online, although a traditional bound version will do nicely in this case. Textbooks often contain useful surveys of a topic, and they also offer bibliographies. Chapters and timelines will give a broad treatment of colonial U.S. history, with less attention to the environment. Check textbook bibliographies for further references.

1G Conduct a General Search on the Internet

Most scholars with access to a computer will supplement a research project by using a high-quality search engine such as Google, located at http://www.google.com. Enter your keywords in the search box and Google "looks" for them on the Internet. Google then takes cached copies or "snapshots" of each relevant page and reports them back to you, in order of their relevance. Google determines relevance by weighing factors that may not be relevant to historical research, such as the number of links to a site.

Search by choosing distinctive keywords. In some cases, you might want to cast a wide net and search for a general term. In other cases, you might want to search for specific names and titles. Let us begin our search on colonial environmental history by simply entering the phrase "William Bartram" in the search box. (Google search results now vary from person to person, depending on one's previous searches.) In my own search for William Bartram, Google unearths quite a few websites that appear to be helpful.

1H Scan the Search Results

How do scholars know which websites are most promising? The list of titles on the first page of the search results may be evaluated by asking what sort of institution publishes the website. The author should represent a reputable institution that is interested in the dissemination of objective information. The institution's administration should support the Internet site and oversee its content. If that is not the case, and the website is published to entertain, make money, or spread disinformation, it must be approached more cautiously. A quick way to learn about an institution publishing a website is to examine the domain name, the abbreviation that occurs after the institution's name. Websites that contain .edu, .ac, and .gov were created by people affiliated with academic and government institutions. At the very least, the authors of the sites had to be accepted or hired by the institution. At most, these websites represent the institution's official views. It must be noted that it is very easy to obtain a domain name ending in org, .net, .com, and .co; anybody with a credit card may do so. These websites tend to be either commercial or personal, which means history students must treat them with great skepticism.

11 Get a Quick First Impression

The first click on a Google search result will reveal much about the reliability of the site. Here are criteria to help you arrive at a quick, critical assessment of our search for William Bartram on Google.

1. Who Is the Author? The more you know about the author, the more likely it is that he or she is willing to stake a reputation on the contents. When an author is identified, do a follow-up search on the name, in order to verify credentials and affiliations. Is the author an authority on the subject of the Internet site?

2. Has the Website Also Been Published in Print? Many sites began as print sources or are published in both print and electronic editions. In these cases the quality is likely to be higher because printed information tends to have higher costs and therefore higher quality controls. Typically, it takes a great deal of time and effort to publish a printed book or journal article. Works of history that are published in these ways usually must meet with the approval of editors and peer reviewers before they are printed and distributed. For this reason, many students have gotten into the habit of trusting printed sources. By contrast, publishing on the Internet can be done cheaply and quickly, often with no controls for quality. There are virtually no barriers to publishing one's own website.

Figure 1.5

3. Is the Information on the Website Available in Hard Copy? There are now many outstanding websites published by historical archives. In these cases, it would be possible to travel to the archives to verify the information that is published online.

4. What Is the Tone of the Website? To a degree, objectivity may be determined by the website's tone. Many websites are written to entertain viewers or to advocate a particular point of view. Other websites are more objective but written with a different audience in mind, say, readers who are young, or who are aficionados and hobbyists. Assessing the tone of a website can be an important component of a preliminary evaluation.

5. Does the Website Feature References? In historical scholarship, it is important for others to be able to follow in an author's footsteps.

This allows us to confirm or contradict an author's findings. If there are no references, it is difficult to verify the information. It may not be reliable and therefore should not be used in a historical essay.

1J Critically Assess Sources on the Internet

Let us now assess the websites that our Google search uncovered for William Bartram. Some of these sources are promising, but others are not.

1. "William Bartram," from Wikipedia, the Free Encyclopedia. Wikipedia is now being used as a first point of reference by many history students because the first page of Google search results often references Wikipedia articles. Wikipedia is an Internet encyclopedia whose articles are written by thousands of volunteer contributors. Contributors may help to revise, update, and edit articles to ensure quality, but there is no board of editors to verify accuracy. Wikipedia contains mistakes. It is for this reason that some history instructors prohibit their students from citing it as a source in their assignments. Other instructors have taken the opposite approach: they have encouraged their students to contribute to Wikipedia to make it better. Still, it is best not to cite Wikipedia in a formal writing assignment. Reading a Wikipedia article, like reading an encyclopedia article, affords a superficial orientation to a subject. Good research requires more of the researcher. In the case of the Wikipedia article about Bartram, it contains good descriptions of basic aspects of his life, plus links to further websites. This information will have to be checked carefully and more will need to be found in other sources.

2. The Travels of William Bartram. This is the official website of an organization called the Bartram Trail Conference. According to the website, the members work to preserve sites linked to Bartram's travels and generally encourage the study of his life. The website contains useful links to sites related to his itineraries and discoveries. There are not many sources here for a student research paper, but with any luck you may one day make an informed visit to some of these sites, which include beautiful locations in the former territory of the Cherokee, Creek, Choctaw, and Seminole.

3. William Bartram. This is a short biography of Bartram. On superficial inspection, the site seems to contain detailed information, which increases its credibility. Even so, the author's name is not given, only an email address to a commercial site. Therefore, this site should be treated with skepticism. Besides, there are many other biographies of Bartram available, so this one does not need to be relied on.

4. William Bartram. This, too, is a commercial website about William Bartram, although in this case it promotes travel and tourism in North Georgia at sites pertaining to him. Once again, the commercial orientation of the site and its duplication of information easily found elsewhere should lead you to ignore it and move on to the next sources.

5. Images for William Bartram. A general search on Google will turn up images related to the man. For a search dedicated completely to imagery, click Images in the top left corner of the Google screen. There are many images of Bartram, as well as reproductions of his illustrations. These may be worth analyzing for the purposes of the research paper. Browse the images, but take the same critical approach as with images on the Internet. Rely on reputable websites affiliated with recognizable, professional institutions, such as libraries and museums.

6. New Georgia Encyclopedia: William Bartram in Georgia. Click this link, which turns out to be an article about Bartram in the *New Georgia Encyclopedia*. It is very easy to check on the quality of this website. One click on the encyclopedia's home page reveals that it is supported by the Georgia Humanities Council, collaborating with the University of Georgia Press and the state's governor's office, among others. These are all established institutions. And at the end of the article is the name of the author, Edward J. Cashin, from Augusta State University. Search on Google for "edward cashin augusta state" and we learn from numerous websites—including one from the *New Georgia Encyclopedia*—that Cashin was a famous expert on Georgia history who died in 2007. For all these reasons, Cashin's article about Bartram in the *New Georgia Encyclopedia* is highly trustworthy. It is also aimed at future researchers. Cashin included a bibliography of ten books, which will help you develop your research.

1K Speak with a Librarian

Librarians are the unsung heroes of the historical world. Historians depend on librarians heavily, and together with librarians historians share a commitment to preserving information. Librarians know how to organize that information and can therefore help historians find things. When in doubt, ask a librarian. College and public librarians have been in the forefront of efforts to organize and make available online information. They usually can offer help with online searching, too.

1L Speak with Your Professor

None of the criteria already listed can be used as the sole determinant of a website's reliability. Taken together, they can help. If you still have doubts about a historical source that you have found on the Internet or in print, present your source to your professor, even just by sending an email message containing the Internet address of the website in question. It is better to ask about a source before you write the paper than to be asked about it after you have turned in the paper.

1M Approach Your Topic from a Particular Angle

A library at a large university will probably contain more than a thousand items that pertain to colonial U.S. environmental history, and it may also have special collections of manuscripts and artifacts. Even a small library may have several dozen items on the topic. Don't be discouraged; you simply need to bring more focus to your topic.

Think back to the books you have read and the courses you have taken. If you like to read biographies, then you might want to identify individuals like Bartram who made a significant contribution to the field. If you like to read social history, you might wish to explore a topic along the lines of class, gender, or race. You might be partial to the history of a particular place or time period. Keep working in the library and on the Internet until it seems you have a manageable number of resources with which to write an essay on a reasonably focused topic.

1N Browse for More Sources

There is only one way to make an informed choice about a topic: go back to the Internet and to the library stacks, and browse through the potential source materials. Look for both quantity and quality. Are there enough sources to write this paper, or are there so many sources that the topic must be narrowed further? It is also important to consider when your sources were published. Are you finding the most recent scholarship, or do your sources seem old enough to be out of date? Are your sources so old that they are from the period of time you are studying?

It is probably a good idea to start with a narrow base of sources and build it into a broader base. As you search for sources in the library stacks, you will find more clues that will lead you to further sources. Just keep in mind that there are limits to your time, and there are limits to your paper. In the early stages of research, you do not need to find everything.

1O Form a Hypothesis

An essay based on historical research should reach new conclusions about a topic. This is a challenging proposition, and by now you may be wondering if it is worth writing a paper about colonial U.S. environmental history at all. Cronon and his fellow scholars have already written plenty about the subject. Can you bring a unique perspective to bear on the topic?

While you are identifying a topic, you should begin forming a hypothesis, one of the most important steps in writing a research paper. A hypothesis is not an ordinary question; it is the question that can guide you through the research. As you read through your sources you will ask for answers to your hypothesis, and as you get answers you will refine your hypothesis. As you do this over the course of your research, you will find that you are getting closer to forming an argument.

How does one arrive at a hypothesis? Start to jot down some questions. In the case of your research focusing on William Bartram, you may be wondering about several things: (1) What sort of person was

Bartram? (2) What distinguished Bartram's travels from other scientists' journeys? (3) How scientific were colonial naturalists? (4) Was Bartram a lone genius, or did he have collaborators?

Now ask yourself two more things: Can you build an argument around the potential answer to one of the questions, and does the question address some broader issue in history? Questions 1 and 2 might yield only descriptions and not arguments. Question 3 could produce a debate (yes, Bartram was a serious scientist; no, he wasn't so serious), but such a debate, although it might have been important during the eighteenth century, would not occur today among historians. Question 4 seems a bit more promising. It could help you ask questions about the social dimensions of scientific research, a common approach for a historian. It would also be interesting to know if Bartram's knowledge derived from Native Americans.

1P Craft a Proposal

After you have completed your preliminary research, craft a one-page proposal. Your teachers and friends will probably be happy to read it and comment on it. Even if they are not, the process of writing the proposal will still help you sketch out your ideas. The proposal is an early opportunity to think critically about your topic.

Every proposal should answer these questions:

1. What is your topic? Describe it briefly.

2. What is your hypothesis? Tell which question is driving your research.

3. What will your readers learn from this project? Will you be bringing new information to light, or will you be interpreting commonplace knowledge in a new way?

4. Why is your project significant or interesting? Discuss the relationship between your project and some broader issue in history.

5. What are your principal sources? Give a short bibliography.

6. What methods will you use to evaluate your sources? Will you be reading library books, or will you be using archival materials? Will you be analyzing objects and paintings? Are any of

your sources in foreign languages, and if so, can you understand them? Will you be using methods from another discipline, such as sociology?

10 Write an Annotated Bibliography

Your object at the next stage of your project should be to compile an annotated bibliography. This exercise will help you assess the breadth and significance of your sources. Arrange your sources according to the instructions for a bibliography given at the end of Chapter 3 of this volume. (For fine examples of annotated bibliographies, see the Oxford Bibliographies Online.) After each entry in your bibliography, summarize the source and state why you will be using it in your paper. You should keep your notes on sources concise, but you may wish to say more about some sources than others; about 150 words will do for each entry. The summaries should address four questions:

1. What type of source is it: a book, a journal article, a historical document?

2. What is the main argument of the source?

3. What evidence is presented by the source?

4. How is the source relevant to your research project?

11 Talk to People About Your Topic

Don't be bashful. Talk with other people about your topic, including your teachers and friends. It can also be interesting to seek out experts in your area of interest. Experts are usually happy to discuss specific research problems with other researchers, especially when they are presented with thoughtful questions and written proposals. If the experts happen to be history professors, visit them during their office hours, or make appointments to see them. You may also wish to seek out experts in other departments of a university, and outside of universities, too. For example, if you were to conduct research on Bartram, you might wish to write to some of the authors working in the field. You might also try to visit key sites that pertain to Bartram's *Travels*.

1S If You Have to Abandon a Topic, Do It Early

The process of finding sources, forming a hypothesis, and crafting a proposal will test the viability of your topic. If at the end of a week or two you no longer want to work on your topic, then find another one. There are plenty of reasons to stop working on a topic; you may not find enough sources, or you may decide that the topic is less interesting than you thought. It is better to bail out of a bad project early than to go down in flames later.

∽ REVIEW ∽

1. Find a topic that interests you.
2. Mine your library for print and online sources.
3. Read bibliographies to find more sources.
4. Make sure your sources are appropriate.
5. Read to develop a hypothesis and craft a proposal.

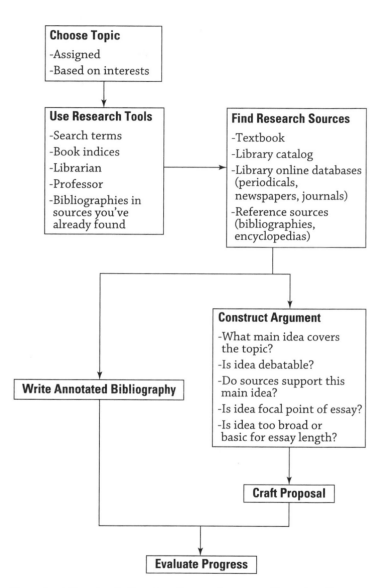

Flowchart Chapter 1 Constructing an Argument Based on Sources

2 Interpreting Source Materials

When you write history, you will know that the sources all relate to a particular topic, but you will have to decide how to interpret and assemble them. At first you might find the sources confusing and even contradictory. Historical writing resembles detective work because sources often raise more questions than they answer. Sometimes they lead historians on an exhilarating wild-goose chase that culminates in a dead end. Other times they enable historians to slowly recover unexpected tales from the past. Fortunately there are many ways to assess source materials.

2A Distinguish Primary Sources from Secondary Works

Sources drive all histories, but not all sources are created equal. As a matter of convenience, historians distinguish between primary sources and secondary works.

1. Primary Sources. Primary sources originate in the time period that historians are studying. They vary a great deal. They may include personal memoirs, government documents, transcripts of legal proceedings, oral histories and traditions, archaeological and biological evidence, and visual sources such as paintings and photographs, as well as translations of sources from their original language. It is likely that these types of primary sources will be very important to your project.

Each kind of primary source must be considered on its own terms. Historians used to think that some source materials were inherently more reliable than others. Leopold von Ranke, the founder of modern, professional history, considered government documents to be the gold standard of all primary sources. But even government documents are subjective in some way. Like all sources, they reveal some things but remain silent on others.

2. Secondary Works. Secondary works reflect on earlier times. Typically, they are books and articles by writers who are interpreting the events and primary sources that you are studying. Secondary works vary a great deal, from books by professional scholars to journalistic accounts. Evaluate each secondary work on its own merits, particularly on how well it uses primary sources as evidence.

This distinction between primary sources and secondary works may be confusing in some cases. If you are writing about historical writers, you may find yourself using a secondary work as a primary source. For example, during the 1840s and 1850s Thomas Babington Macaulay wrote *The History of England*; his book describes the origins and outcome of England's Glorious Revolution of 1688. For historians of seventeenth-century England, Macaulay's book is a classic secondary work. But for historians of Victorian Britain, *The History of England* is a rich primary source that tells historians a great deal about intellectual life in the 1840s and 1850s.[1]

2B Refine Your Hypothesis with Who, What, Why, Where, and When

While you are reading each source, you should be asking how the source might support or contradict your hypothesis. Pretty soon, you will have a lot of information that relates to your hypothesis. Organize your answers around the journalist's questions of who, what, why, where, when.

Journalists tell beginning reporters to ask these questions when they are reporting a story. Historian Richard Marius began his career as a journalist, and in his *Short Guide to Writing About History* he advises students to ask these reporter's questions when they read source materials. It is good advice. Answers to these questions can be very complex, depending on the sources and the story.[2]

Take notes and use your answers to help you form ideas for your essay.

Imagine for a moment that you are writing a biography of George Washington, and that your sources consist mainly of eighteenth-century archival materials. To get through these sources, you have formed a hypothesis: that Washington was a weak leader who made many poor decisions, some of which are still controversial. As you read about all of Washington's decisions, consider organizing your research around the reporter's questions. Once you start to get answers, take notes.

The *Who* Question. Historians ask "who" to learn biographical information about significant actors, to learn who bore the brunt of historical changes, and to learn who caused things to happen. In your biography of Washington, you could use the sources to make yourself familiar with all the main characters. Who were Washington's family members, and did they support his decisions? Who supported Washington when he commanded the Continental Army? Who opposed him?

The *What* Question. Different sources often describe the same events differently. Know each version of events so that you can compare accounts. Let us say that you are focusing momentarily on Washington's decision to cross the Delaware. What did Washington know about the strength of the British forces? What did his troops do to surprise the Hessian troops on the other side of the river? What were the strategic and political consequences of Washington's decision?

The *Why* Question. Why did some things change while others remained the same? Using each source, make a list of possible causes. Try to distinguish the most significant causes of events from the background causes. Why did a responsible Virginia planter like Washington decide to rebel against the king of England? Did he support independence because his farm would be more likely to prosper without British trade restrictions? Or did he truly believe in representative government? Why did Washington accept the command of the Continental Army? Did he want to serve his new country, or did he simply enjoy the trappings of power?

The *Where* Question. Sometimes you will find fairly self-evident answers to the *where* question. Other times, geographical considerations will open your eyes to unexpected circumstances. You might even find it helpful to draw a map of your subject. Where, for example, is Valley Forge? Was it a wise idea for Washington to ask his troops to spend the winter in such a cold, miserable place? Where else could they have gone, given the problems of transportation in eighteenth-century America, and given the location of British forces?

The *When* Question. Historians analyze change and continuity over time. Not surprisingly, it becomes quite important to know when historical events happened. Depending on the topic, you may get an easy answer or no answer at all. Try as much as you can to determine when things happened. Use this information to place events in a chronological relationship. Try to make one timeline from all your source materials so that you may understand the order of events. When, for example, did Washington decide to attack the British General Cornwallis at Yorktown? Could he have won the war sooner rather than later, or did too much depend on timely assistance from the French army and navy?

2C Be Sensitive to Points of View in Your Sources

As you use your hypothesis to work your way through the source materials, you will come to see that many sources present history from a certain point of view. Even photographs show only the perspective of the photographer. Photographers have even been known to arrange their pictures so as to "edit" the overall story being told, and their mere presence with a camera changes how their subjects behave. How then do historians know which sources to trust?

Historians must be sensitive to how sources come to be available. Why is only some information available? Chroniclers record events as they happen, but they describe only the things they consider to be important. For example, in a book called *Silencing the Past*, Michel-Rolph Trouillot mentions that Caribbean slave owners usually kept detailed records of their plantations, but sometimes the slave owners neglected to record births. Infant mortality was so high on some plantations that it was not worth the trouble to add a new slave child to the registers until the baby survived to a certain age. Therefore, these records lack important data. Historians may wish to reconstruct the history of Caribbean slave families, but the plantation chronicles make it a difficult task. Chroniclers use their own contemporary standards when they decide to record certain events and to keep silent about others.[3]

The process of producing sources does not end with the selections of the chroniclers. All sorts of factors determine whether or not chronicles will survive. Sometimes wars, fires, and floods can silence the past. But most of the time, collectors, archivists, and librarians decide to preserve some chronicles and to discard others. They have their own visions of the past, and politics and economics can influence their decisions in many ways. For example, during the 1960s Loren Graham began to collect information about a Soviet engineer named Peter Palchinsky, who was executed by Stalin in 1929. Graham believed that Palchinsky had made significant contributions to early Soviet engineering, but the Soviet government was hiding Palchinsky's papers from researchers because the engineer had criticized the regime. Graham had to wait almost thirty years, but when the Soviet Union collapsed he finally gained access to Palchinsky's papers. Then, in a nice twist of fate, Graham found that the papers could help him write a book that explained, in part, the Soviet Union's failure. His quest for sources became a subplot of his history *The Ghost of the Executed Engineer*.[4] But even in Graham's case, the selections of chroniclers influenced the writing of history.

2D Select the Most Important Source Materials

You cannot include everything in your essay. You must select the information that you need to make your point, even if this means neglecting potentially interesting tangents. Historians are not just collectors of facts; they are selectors and arrangers. They function like the human memory, remembering some things and forgetting others. Try not to be like the main character in Jorge Luis Borges's story "Funes, the Memorious":

> He remembered the shapes of the clouds in the south at dawn on the 30th of April of 1882, and he could compare them in his recollection with the marbled grain in the design of a leatherbound book which he had seen only once, and with the lines in the spray which an oar raised in the Rio Negro on the eve of the battle of Quebracho. . . . He told me . . . *My memory, sir, is like a garbage disposal.*[5]

Historians exercise selectivity with sources so that they may avoid producing garbage disposals. Some information will be significant to an essay, but much will be insignificant. Don't feel bad if you spend a lot of time interpreting a source, only to find that it does not contribute to your essay's main idea. It is tempting to include such sources, if only to show your readers how hard you have been working, but some sources are bound to be irrelevant. In the end, a coherent essay will impress readers more than a garbage disposal.

2E Take Notes by Being Selective

When you first begin to analyze your sources, you will need to take notes. When historians take notes, they take advantage of a number of techniques: some use index cards and notebook paper, while others use word-processing programs or even database programs. Choosing a method of taking notes depends to a great extent on the type of research you are conducting, and it is often a matter of personal preference. As you conduct more research, you will get a better sense of how you prefer to take notes.

All note-taking methods, whether low-tech or high-tech, present a common difficulty: how to select the most important material for your notes. Usually, you do not want to copy your sources word for word. You want to write down only the information that is likely to be useful in your essay. But how do you know what is going to be useful before you even write the essay? Reaching this decision is the most difficult part of note taking. You want to write down useful information, but you recognize that some information appearing to be useless now may turn out to be useful later.

It is difficult to know in advance which notes will be useful. It is for this reason that you should use your hypothesis to help you read sources. Ask yourself how a source relates to your hypothesis, and jot down notes from the source that answer fundamental questions about your hypothesis. Use your hypothesis to help select the most important information from your sources.

The trickiest thing about using a hypothesis during note taking is that your hypothesis is likely to change. This is as it should be. Over the course of your research, you will refine your ideas about your sources, and your hypothesis will get closer and closer to a thesis or argument. Unfortunately, this also means that your early notes will be more extensive and less useful than your later notes. Don't be disappointed if, at the end of a project, you find that you have taken some extraneous notes; it is a natural consequence of refining a hypothesis and being selective.

⌘ REVIEW ⌘

1. *Think* as you read.
2. Question your sources.
3. Be aware of sources' points of view.
4. Take notes that are relevant to your hypothesis.

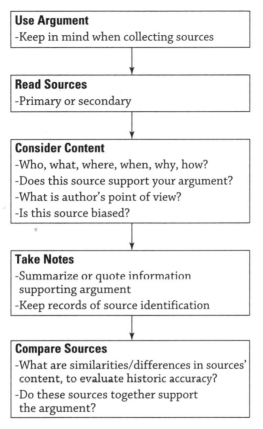

Use Argument
-Keep in mind when collecting sources

Read Sources
-Primary or secondary

Consider Content
-Who, what, where, when, why, how?
-Does this source support your argument?
-What is author's point of view?
-Is this source biased?

Take Notes
-Summarize or quote information
 supporting argument
-Keep records of source identification

Compare Sources
-What are similarities/differences in sources'
 content, to evaluate historic accuracy?
-Do these sources together support
 the argument?

Flowchart Chapter 2 Taking Notes

3 Writing History Faithfully

In the first century BCE, Cicero said, "The first law for the historian is that he shall never dare utter an untruth. The second is that he shall suppress nothing that is true."[1] The spirit of these laws remains the same, even if some of the conventions for writing history have changed—such as the present convention for writing in language that is gender-neutral.

Good historical writers always question authorities, even formidable ones like Cicero. One question comes immediately to mind: How do historians know what is true? They may never know the answer to such a question because sources often present contradictions and silences. Even so, historians recognize certain rules of representing the past faithfully. Like the law, these rules are written down but are also subject to variation and interpretation over time. Historians do not take a Hippocratic oath to uphold any particular body of rules, yet a broad consensus exists among historical writers about what is right and what is wrong.

3A Collect and Report Your Sources Carefully

There is more to honesty than simply having good intentions. Historians must be faithful to sources by collecting and reporting them carefully. Scholarship relies heavily on trust because scholars all build on the work of others. Above all, it is important to report accurately on the people and events of the past.

Sloppy note taking can cause you to misrepresent history. Even if your misrepresentations are inadvertent, readers may still accuse you of dishonesty. To avoid any such misunderstanding, apply some basic rules to your note taking:

1. Every Note Should Contain a Citation. Every time you jot down a note, write the bibliographic reference next to it. Every note card, computer entry, and piece of paper should indicate where you got the information. Always include page numbers. If you are pressed for time, do not cut corners in your notes; work out a system of abbreviations. This will help later, too, when you may need to look back for a specific quote that suits your argument.

3A

2. Make a Clear Distinction Between Your Words and Your Source's Words. Always put direct quotations in quotation marks. When you paraphrase someone else's words, make sure your own words are distinct.

3. Watch Your Word Processor. Ages ago, when historians wrote with quill pens and typewriters, writing and revising drafts was a painful process. The smallest alterations made it necessary to rewrite or retype the entire manuscript. Nowadays, word processing makes it easier to compose and revise while you consult sources. This is convenient, but word processors do present some organizational challenges. Always keep your notes in a separate file from your writing. Be especially careful when cutting and pasting source materials from the Internet. If you keep notes and text in the same file, you will run the risk of confusing your own words with someone else's. Writing technology has changed, but the standards for evaluating plagiarism have remained the same.[2]

4. Consider Using Online Organizers. The introduction of word-processing software made it easier to write and revise history. It sped up note taking, too, but it did not change the organization of notes. Historians sometimes use database and spreadsheet software to keep track of information. Increasingly, historians are turning to online project management software to organize research and note taking. There are several types of software available, and one program has been developed with historians in mind. The Center for History and New Media at George Mason University has created a program called Zotero, which helps historians collect, organize, and cite their sources. The program plugs into conventional web-browsing and word-processing software and is available for free at http://www.zotero.org.

3B Incorporate the Ideas of Others with Care and Respect

When you conduct research and write papers, you will have to engage the ideas of fellow scholars. Much of the time you will be interpreting subjects that others have interpreted before you. Even if you are the first person to write a history of something, chances are you will have to place your own ideas in the context of a broader historical literature.

All historians know that writing is hard work. Therefore it is important to acknowledge the work of others respectfully. Historians have conventions for quoting, summarizing, and paraphrasing the works of other scholars. Keep these conventions in mind while you are taking notes; that way you will not have to go back and check your sources while you are writing.

3C Know the Difference Between Summaries and Paraphrases

Technically speaking, a paraphrase restates another writer's words in about the same number of words; a summary reduces another writer's words to a more concise number of words. Historical writers often paraphrase and summarize the ideas of others. Paraphrase when you think it is important to discuss someone else's work but you think you can say the same thing more clearly in about the same number of words. Summarize when you think you can say it more clearly and more concisely, or when the longer version is inappropriate. A summary or a paraphrase indicates to your reader that you have digested another author's work to the point where you can restate it in your own words.

In historical writing, paraphrasing is not as common as summarizing, but paraphrasing still has its uses. This is particularly helpful when you must translate an archaic or complex quotation into standard English. For example, in *To Keep and Bear Arms: The Origins of an Anglo-American Right*, historian Joyce Malcolm analyzes passages from William Blackstone's *Commentaries on the Laws of England*, the eighteenth century's most famous interpretation of the law. Blackstone wrote, "In a land of liberty, it is extremely dangerous to make a distinct order of the profession of arms." Malcolm precedes this slightly archaic quotation with her own paraphrase: "As for standing armies, Blackstone recommended they be treated with utmost caution."[3] Malcolm's paraphrase helps readers understand Blackstone's somewhat old-fashioned terminology.

A summary of someone else's work is usually more convenient than a paraphrase because historians write to express their own original ideas, even when they are engaging the ideas of others. Summaries are everywhere in historical writing, most commonly in works of synthesis. In a survey of colonial American social history, *Pursuits of Happiness*, Jack Greene summarizes the work of Perry Miller, an earlier historian who wrote some classic studies of New England:

> Although, as Perry Miller has emphasized, New England religious culture remained vital and adaptable throughout the years from 1670 to 1730, it lost its former preeminence in community life.

Greene then summarizes some of Miller's evidence in a few more brisk sentences. Even though Miller's work was both stimulating and extensive, Greene has a limited amount of space to devote to it. Still, he has given a fair summary. Readers who want to know more about Miller may use Greene's citations as a guide to further reading.[4]

3D Learn How and When to Quote

Most often, historians demonstrate their familiarity with sources by summarizing and paraphrasing, but occasionally they find that a direct quotation is the best way to make a point. Use a direct quotation when the language of your source is vivid and you cannot possibly do justice to it by summarizing or paraphrasing it. Also quote a source directly when key points of interpretation depend on the exact wording in the source. Otherwise, try to limit your use of quotations. Readers are reading your writing principally to find out your own original ideas.

There are two kinds of quotations. Most of the time when historians quote, they run the quotation into their own text. Typically, they begin the sentence by telling the reader who is speaking; then they insert the quotation. Imagine that you are writing about the nineteenth-century French philosopher Pierre Joseph Proudhon. You write,

> At a time when the French middle classes were growing, Proudhon was quite brave to declare that "property is theft."

Notice that in this sentence it was not necessary to separate the body of the sentence from the quotation by using a comma or a colon. These punctuation marks should be used with a quotation only when the punctuation is necessary for the grammar and syntax of the sentence.

The second kind of quotation is called a block quotation. When it is necessary to quote a passage that is longer than three lines, they indent five spaces from the left margin and type the quotation in a block set off from the text. The sentence before the quotation should introduce it; the sentence after the quotation should link it to the text that follows. For example, in his pioneering social history *The Making of the English Working Class*, E. P. Thompson used block quotations to give readers a flavor of English discourse on the subject of labor during the late eighteenth century and early nineteenth century. Thompson used the words of the activist Francis Place to define some key terms. Thompson wrote:

> Such diversity of experiences has led some writers to question both the notions of an "industrial revolution" and of a "working class." The first discussion need not detain us here. The term is serviceable enough in its usual connotations. For the second, many writers prefer the term working *classes*, which emphasises the great disparity in status, acquisitions, skills,

conditions within the portmanteau phrase. And in this they echo the complaints of Francis Place:

> If the character and the conduct of the working people are to be taken from reviews, magazines, pamphlets, newspapers, reports of the two Houses of Parliament and the Factory Commissioners, we shall find them all jumbled together as the "lower orders," the most skilled and the most prudent workman, with the most igno- rant and imprudent laborers and paupers, though the difference is great indeed, and indeed in many cases will scarce admit of comparison.

Place is, of course, right: the Sunderland tailor, the Irish navvy, the Jewish costermonger, the inmate of an East Anglian village workhouse, the compositor on *The Times*—all might be seen by their "betters" as belonging to the "lower classes" while they themselves might scarcely understand each other's dialect.[5]

Thompson connects his own ideas to the ideas of Place by seamlessly integrating the block quotation with the preceding and following paragraphs. Thompson uses the quote as a vivid illustration of a point. Most historians use block quotations, but they tend to use them spar- ingly. Too many block quotations tend to diminish the author's own voice, while summaries and paraphrases highlight an author's skills at analysis.

3E   Use Ellipses and Brackets, But Do Justice to Your Sources

When historians insert quotations in their writing, they often abridge the quotation so that it reflects the needs of their own writ- ing more precisely. Historians indicate these changes by marks of ellipsis, which look like three periods (. . .) and also by using square brackets like these: [ ]. One basic rule governs the use of ellipses and brackets: any abridged quotation must be faithful to the original, full quotation.

This is not as easy as it sounds. Marks of ellipsis and brackets can be tricky to use faithfully. Imagine that you are writing a five-page essay about Thomas Jefferson's "Declaration of Independence." You have decided to analyze Jefferson's complaints about how King George III treated the American colonial legislatures. Jefferson enumerated these complaints:

- He has refused his Assent to Laws, the most wholesome and necessary for the Public Good.
- He has forbidden his Governors to pass laws of immediate and pressing importance, unless suspended in their operation till his Assent should be obtained; and when so suspended, he has utterly neglected to attend to them.
- He has refused to pass other Laws for the accommodation of large districts of people, unless those people would relinquish the right of Representation in the Legislature, a right inestimable to them and formidable to tyrants only.
- He has called together legislative bodies at places unusual, uncomfortable, and distant from the depository of their Public Records, for the sole purpose of fatiguing them into compliance with his measures.
- He has dissolved Representative Houses repeatedly, for opposing with manly firmness his invasions on the rights of the people.
- He has refused for a long time, after such dissolutions, to cause others to be elected; whereby the Legislative Powers, incapable of Annihilation, have returned to the People at large for their exercise; the State remaining in the meantime exposed to all the dangers of invasion from without, and convulsions within.

Jefferson's language is unique and vivid; therefore you wish to use quotations to support your point. But as much as you would like to quote Jefferson in full, you are writing a short essay, and a full quotation would take up too much space. For this reason, you decide to convey Jefferson's main points by abridging his writing with marks of ellipsis:

> Jefferson listed five complaints about the ways in which King George III treated the colonial legislatures: "He has refused his Assent to Laws . . . He has forbidden his Governors to pass laws of immediate and pressing importance . . . He has refused to pass other Laws for the accommodation of large

districts of people . . . He has called together legislative bodies at places unusual . . . He has dissolved Representative Houses repeatedly . . . He has refused for a long time . . . to cause others to be elected . . ."

But notice that your sentence does not flow well into the quotation: there is a jarring difference between your verb tense and Jefferson's. You could eliminate the problem by removing the word "has," except that you would be stuck with the incorrect form of the verb "to forbid." In addition, writing "King George" and then having the quotation repeat "he" as the subject sounds unnatural. To solve these problems, you may wish to insert some bracketed words so that your sentence flows naturally into the quotation from Jefferson. The brackets say to your readers that these are not Jefferson's exact words, but they still convey Jefferson's exact meaning. You may decide to write:

3E

> Jefferson listed five complaints about how King George III treated the colonial legislatures, namely that he "refused his Assent to Laws . . . [forbade] his Governors to pass laws of immediate and pressing importance . . . refused to pass other Laws for the accommodation of large districts of people . . . called together legislative bodies at places unusual . . . dissolved Representative Houses repeatedly . . . [and] refused for a long time . . . to cause others to be elected . . . "

This quotation is faithful to Jefferson's exact meaning, even though it abridges his quotation with ellipses and brackets. It would have been unfaithful to use ellipses in this manner: "He has refused to pass other Laws for the accommodation of large districts of people . . . for the sole purpose of fatiguing them into compliance with his measures." This would be unfair to Jefferson, because the first portion of the original quotation was followed by an entirely different set of ideas: "unless those people would relinquish the right of Representation in the Legislature, a right inestimable to them and formidable to tyrants only."

It also would have been unfaithful to Jefferson to use brackets this way: "He has forbidden his Governors to pass [important] laws . . ." This changes the sense of the original quotation, "He has forbidden his Governors to pass laws of immediate and pressing importance . . ."

If you need to be so concise, summarizing Jefferson in your own words would be preferable to inserting different words directly into Jefferson's original writing.

3F Learn How to Use Quotation Marks

After apostrophes, quotation marks probably cause more confusion than any other form of punctuation. This is partly because American practice differs from British practice. Most of us probably read historical works from all over the English-speaking world. When it comes to your own writing you may indeed have grounds for confusion.

1. American Style for Quotation Marks. When you run a quotation into your text, place the words of the quotation inside double quotation marks:

> Eisenhower warned against the "military-industrial complex."

For a quotation within a quotation, use single quotation marks:

> In his history of the Space Age, *The Heavens and the Earth*, Walter MacDougall writes that Eisenhower feared "the assumption of inordinate power and influence by a 'military-industrial complex' and a 'scientific-technological elite.'"[6]

Notice also how the other forms of punctuation are placed in relation to the quotation marks. Periods and commas should be placed *inside* the quotation marks. If you use question marks and exclamation points, place them inside the quotation marks only when they formed part of the original quotation. If you are adding your own question marks and exclamation points after the quotation, then place them outside the quotation marks. Colons and semicolons also go outside the quotation marks.

2. British Style for Quotation Marks. The British use quotation marks in the opposite way from Americans. When a quotation is run into the text, the words of the quotation are placed in single quotation marks:

> Eisenhower warned against the 'military-industrial complex'.

For a quotation within a quotation, double quotation marks are used:

> In his history of the Space Age, Walter MacDougall writes that Eisenhower feared 'the assumption of inordinate power and influence by a "military-industrial complex" and a "scientific-technological elite"'.[7]

Notice also that in British usage all other punctuation marks are placed *outside* the quotation marks.

3G Don't Plagiarize

Historians find unfaithful quotations disturbing, but they reserve the harshest condemnation for plagiarists. In the ancient Mediterranean world, *plagiarii* were pirates who kidnapped young children, among other misdeeds.[8] When plagiarists claim someone else's ideas as their own they steal someone else's brainchild. And contrary to folk wisdom, there is no honor among thieves. Historians do not tolerate plagiarists. Universities punish them.

Cases of plagiarism happen infrequently because there is such a powerful consensus against it. It is so pleasurable to share ideas honestly and to write history faithfully that real historians should never feel an urge to plagiarize. Historians share this commitment to honesty with writers across all the disciplines.

1. Direct Plagiarism. Direct plagiarism occurs when one writer takes another writer's exact words and passes them off as his or her own. Direct plagiarism is very easy for an informed reader to spot.

2. Indirect Plagiarism. Indirect plagiarism is more difficult to recognize and it is also more insidious. Indirect plagiarism occurs when writers paraphrase someone else's work too closely. The basic structure of the sentence or paragraph is retained, and the plagiarist substitutes an occasional new word or phrase to make the writing slightly different. For example, here is an original passage taken from Thomas Holt's book about emancipated slaves in Jamaica, *The Problem of Freedom*. Holt writes:

> Presiding over this sparkling court was Elizabeth Vassall Fox, who had inherited her estates in 1800 from her grandfather

> Florentius Vassall. Yet Lady Holland was as staunch a Whig as
> her husband and shared many of his libertarian sentiments.[9]

The following passage is an overly close paraphrase that would be an example of indirect plagiarism:

> Elizabeth Vassall Fox presided over this brilliant court. In 1800,
> she had inherited several plantations from her grandfather, and
> yet, like her husband, she was a Whig and a libertarian.

And the following paragraph would be indirect plagiarism even if the author gave a citation to Holt. The paraphrase is too close to Holt's original text to be considered the author's original writing.

> This salon was led by Elizabeth Vassall Fox, also known as Lady
> Holland. She was a noted Whig and libertarian whose family
> fortune derived from plantation slavery.

3. Inadvertent Plagiarism. What if you accidentally forget to put quotation marks around a passage from someone else's writing? What if you forget to provide a citation when you summarize someone else's writing? Think for a minute about your audience. When they read your work, all they see are the words in front of them. They do not see how you were frantically putting your essay together at two in the morning. By the time you tell them that you were in a rush and made some mistakes, they will not care. When your readers detect a misstep on your part, they will instinctively form the worst possible impression of you.

Recently, two popular historians, Stephen Ambrose and Doris Kearns Goodwin, have had to defend themselves against plagiarism: they have admitted to sloppy research practices. This is a common defense against charges of plagiarism. It is also an embarrassing way to defend oneself. In the case of Ambrose and Goodwin, the "sloppiness" defense highlights the relationship between plagiarism and lack of self-discipline. Historians must avoid situations that may be conducive to plagiarism. Do not wait until the last minute to research and write historical essays. Be sure that there is plenty of time to document historical sources correctly.

In history you are guilty until proven innocent. To make matters worse, it will be easy for your readers to prove your guilt, and it will be difficult for you to prove your innocence. Perhaps this is not fair, but this is how your audience thinks.

4. Academic Dishonesty. Plagiarism means you are passing off someone else's work as your own. Therefore, it should go without saying that you should not submit an essay someone else wrote for you. This includes buying a paper from a disreputable company on the Internet, or submitting a paper from a fraternity file. If you do these things you are a plagiarist because someone else did your work for you.

There are other acts of academic dishonesty that closely resemble plagiarism. Submitting the same paper in two courses means you are passing off work done in one course as work done in another course. Usually, dual submissions require the permission of both instructors. In addition, an instructor's permission is usually required if you want to submit a paper that you wrote in collaboration with another student. You should not pass off the other student's writing as your own writing. It is usually appropriate for you to discuss a paper assignment with another student, but when it comes to writing, do it alone.

3H Be Honest, But Don't Give Unnecessary Citations

It is conceivable that after reading the preceding section on plagiarism and dishonesty, you will be so frightened that you will provide a citation in every sentence you write. Don't go overboard with citations. Include a citation when you quote directly, when you paraphrase or summarize someone else's ideas, or when you are consciously imitating the structure of someone else's writing. There is no need to give a citation for a piece of information that reasonable people consider to be general knowledge, for example, that the Allies landed at Normandy on June 6, 1944, or that railroads played a significant role in British industrialization. These pieces of information should be obvious to everyone who has studied history. Of course, if you are unsure whether something is common knowledge, play it safe and offer a citation.[10]

31 Choose a Citation System That Suits Your Audience

All scholars agree to use sources responsibly. Two rules apply to all citation systems: be consistent, and make it easy for your readers to check your sources. There is less agreement among scholars about specific formats for citing source materials. This is for a variety of reasons. Some publishers and editors may require special methods for citing sources, and some college instructors may have special requirements, too. For this reason it is important for historians to find out which format their audience expects them to use.

Students sometimes find citing sources to be confusing, often because history instructors have different rules from those of teachers in other disciplines. For example, many social scientists use a system where they place an author's name, date of publication, and page number in parentheses after a quotation, summary, or paraphrase. Sometimes historians find this system suits an essay or book particularly well. Nevertheless, most historians use sequential footnotes or endnotes.

Several guides to citations exist, but there is one that is widely recognized by historians: Kate L. Turabian, *A Manual for Writers of Term Papers, Theses, and Dissertations*, 8th ed. (Chicago: University of Chicago Press, 2013). "Turabian," as it is called, is a shorter version of the rules contained in the *Chicago Manual of Style*, which most historians consider to be the authoritative guide for preparing manuscripts. You will find that historians and their editors usually follow Turabian and the *Chicago Manual* in their professional publications.

Most history instructors prefer that students use footnotes or endnotes, which are easy to create in word-processing programs. The following rules apply to them. For special or unusual circumstances, refer to Turabian or the *Chicago Manual,* both of which can be found in any academic library. The *Chicago Manual* may also be accessed online. Keep in mind that if you choose Zotero software to manage your research and note taking, it will automatically format all your notes for you.

1. Formatting Footnotes and Endnotes on a Word Processor. It is usually possible to format a word-processing program to handle some aspects of noting automatically. Notes should be single-spaced in the same font size as the main text. The first line of the note may begin with an indentation from the left margin, or it may also begin with a hanging indentation. The note number should be written as an arabic numeral. After it, insert a period and a space.

2. Citing a Book. Endnotes and footnotes to books should be written like this:

> 4. Robert K. Massie, *Dreadnought: Britain, Germany, and the Coming of the Great War* (New York: Random House, 1991), 183–85.

Notice what distinguishes a footnote or endnote from a bibliographic entry: in a note, the author's first name comes first, information about the publisher is placed in parentheses, and a comma precedes the page numbers. There is usually no need for a "p." or a "pp." in front of the page numbers, unless there are grounds for confusion with other numbers in the citation. Some electronic books do not feature page numbers. In such cases, cite a chapter or a section, doing your best to guide the reader.

3. Citing Different Kinds of Books. Not all books have such simple publication information. In fact, the possible permutations are endless. Given next are examples of notes for some standard types of books that historical writers often cite: a multiauthor book, a multivolume book, an edited volume, and a revised edition. These four examples (and the others after that) open with made-up numbers as if they are from a list of notes.

> 11. Steven Shapin and Simon Schaffer, *Leviathan and the Air-Pump: Hobbes, Boyle, and the Experimental Life* (Princeton, NJ: Princeton University Press, 1985), 244.
> 12. Noël Deerr, *The History of Sugar*, 2 vols. (London: Chapman and Hall, 1949–50), 2:184.
> 13. *Maroon Societies: Rebel Slave Communities in the Americas*, ed. Richard Price (New York: Anchor Press, 1973), 112–15.
> 14. Roland Oliver and Anthony Atmore, *Africa since 1800* (Cambridge, UK: Cambridge University Press, 1967; 4th ed., 1994), 67.

4. Citing Scholarly Articles. Scholarly articles by historians are usually published in either scholarly journals or edited collections. The form for edited collections resembles a book citation:

> 37. Bernard S. Cohn, "Representing Authority in Victorian India," in *The Invention of Tradition*, ed. Eric Hobsbawm and Terence Ranger (Cambridge, UK: Cambridge University Press, 1983), 169.

Journal articles are cited somewhat differently. The author and title are given, followed by the title of the journal, its volume and number, the date in parentheses, and a colon followed by the page number. Here is a simple citation and then one that is more complex.

> 38. Jessica A. Coope, "Religious and Cultural Conversion to Islam in Ninth-Century Umayyad Córdoba," *Journal of World History* 4, no. 1 (Spring 1993): 63.
>
> 39. Amy Wiese Forbes, "'Let's Add the Stomach': Satire, Absurdity, and July Monarchy Politics in Proudhon's *What Is Property*?" *French Historical Studies* 4, no. 24 (Fall 2001): 681.

Ordinarily, an article title is simply placed in quotation marks, followed by the underlined or italicized journal title, and the publication information. Observe that in the preceding example, we can see special punctuation marks. In the first part of the title, there is a quotation, placed in single quotation marks within the double quotation marks. In the second part of the title, there is a book title, which should be underlined or italicized. And in the second example, we also see that the comma between the article title and the journal title can be dispensed with because the title ends with a question mark.

5. Citing Works of Journalism. Articles in newspapers and magazines may provide less publication information than scholarly articles, but historians should still offer as much information as possible, in the order author, title of article, title of magazine or newspaper, date, and page number. For example,

> 40. Diana Trilling, "A Visit to Camelot," *The New Yorker*, June 2, 1997, 56.

6. Citing the Internet. Standards for citing sources on the Internet have not yet evolved completely. Even so, Internet citations follow the same principles as other citations: they should give readers all the information they need to find a source. Internet citations should give the fullest possible Uniform Resource Locator (URL) address of the source, not just the homepage.

As much as it is important to follow the same principles as with other citations, it is also important to acknowledge that Internet citations differ from print sources. Print sources are usually permanent; they can almost always be located in a major research library. Internet sites may change or disappear.

Should a reader challenge your use of a source, it will be helpful for you to have a saved copy of the Internet site from the day on which you used it. When you consult a website, be sure to give the date of retrieval at the end of the citation. The website may change or even disappear.

There are also minor ways in which the Internet is different for purposes of citation. First you may give conventional citation information, such as author, title, and date of publication. But then you must also give the URL. Complete URLs are desirable, although steps may be taken to avoid URLs longer than two lines.

Let us take a look at a well-known historical website, *Valley of the Shadow: Two Communities in the American Civil War*, edited by Edward Ayers, Anne Rubin, William Thomas, and Andrew Torget. This website contains reproductions of many primary sources, including photographs, letters, and newspaper articles that pertain to the U.S. Civil War. When citing a newspaper article from the *Valley of the Shadow*, here is the method for the first citation:

> 42. "Lincoln's Fiendish Proclamation," *Staunton Spectator*, 7 Oct. 1862, p. 2, col. 1. In "The War Years: Newspapers." *Valley of the Shadow: Two Communities in the American Civil War*, Virginia Center for Digital History, University of Virginia, http://valley.lib.virginia.edu/news/ss1862/va.au.ss.1862.10.07.xml. Accessed Feb. 18, 2011.

7. Citing Films, Television Shows, and Audiovisual Sources. The general principle is to cite the title in italics. Then, in regular type, the name of the director is given, followed by the date. If a DVD recording is being used, the publisher and date should also be given.

> 31. *Lawrence of Arabia*, directed by David Lean (1962; Sony Pictures DVD 2001).

8. Citing Interviews, Lectures, and Oral Presentations. These kinds of citations should give the name of the source and the place and date on which he or she gave you the information. Courtesy dictates that private conversations should not be cited unless you have the permission of the person you interviewed.

> 76. Ernest Hemingway, interview with the author, Key West, Florida, September 6, 1932.

9. Citing Archival Sources. Each archive is organized differently, but citations should be included that will allow readers to trace your sources. Some archives, such as Britain's National Archives (NA), even furnish readers with standard guidelines for citing sources from their collection. Here is a source found in the NA, in the Colonial Office (CO) files labeled number 167:

> 61. Lees to Knutsford, with minutes by Wingfield, Jan. 9, 1891, NA CO 167/661.

If you are conducting research in an archive, be sure to ask if there is a correct way to cite their sources. If not, be sure that your readers understand any abbreviations you may choose to use.

10. Citing Unpublished Secondary Works. Sometimes you will need to cite an unpublished secondary work. It is not unusual to discover useful unpublished theses and dissertations during the course of your research, although you may need to have the author's permission to read or cite one. (Ask the librarian whether you need permission.) Cite theses and dissertations according to this format:

8. Kristen Anne Tegtmeier, "Bleeding Borders: The Intersection of Gender, Race, and Region in Territorial Kansas" (Ph.D. diss., University of Texas at Austin, 2000), 144.

Historians also circulate unpublished papers or manuscripts to each other. Professional courtesy dictates that these may be used and cited only when the author permits it.

33. William K. Storey, "Science and the Making of a British Ideology of Development in Post-Emancipation Barbados" (unpublished manuscript in the author's possession), 14.

11. How to Repeat a Citation Without Using Latin Abbreviations. In the olden days, when historians wanted to cite a work for the second time, they used "ibid." if the citation followed the original citation immediately, and they used "op. cit." and "loc. cit." when the citation came after citations to other works.

No more! The *Chicago Manual* now considers *op. cit.* and *loc. cit.* to be archaic and obsolete. *Ibid.* may still be used, but when you revise an essay by cutting and pasting paragraphs, you may find that using *ibid.* in your notes will make it difficult to keep track of your sources. There is an easier, simpler system for shortening references. The first time you cite a source, give the full citation, but after the first time give an abbreviation: author's last name, abbreviated title, and page number. Here are some examples:

11. Denis Judd, *Empire: The British Imperial Experience from 1765 to the Present* (New York: Basic Books, 1996), 79.
12. Judd, *Empire*, 80.
13. Bruno Latour, *We Have Never Been Modern*, trans. Catherine Porter (Cambridge, MA: Harvard University Press, 1993), 90.
14. Latour, *Never Been Modern*, 91.
15. Judd, *Empire*, 84.
16. Latour, *Never Been Modern*, 91.

12. How to Place a Superscript Note in the Main Text. When you read, notice that most historians place a note at the end of a sentence, not in the middle. Notes in the middle of a sentence are annoying and distracting. They should be used only when they are absolutely necessary to distinguish one person's ideas from another. Here is an example of a poorly placed note: "William McFeely suggests[4] that racism is an insidious problem in American life." The note number really belongs at the end of the sentence, because at that point you are still discussing McFeely and his book *Sapelo's People* (New York: Norton, 1994). The only way it would be appropriate to place the number in the middle of the sentence would be if you had to distinguish McFeely's ideas from someone else's: "William McFeely suggests that racism is an insidious problem in American life,[4] but other writers feel differently."[5]

13. Citing a Quotation of a Quotation. Historians prefer to quote from original sources. If you see a primary source quotation in a secondary work and you want to quote it yourself, check the primary source and assess the accuracy of the quotation. When you go back and find the original primary source, this entitles you to cite the primary source.

Sometimes it may not be possible for you to find the original primary source. In this case, acknowledge the primary source, but say "as cited in" or "as quoted by" the secondary work. Imagine that you are reading about the execution of Louis XVI in Simon Schama's book *Citizens: A Chronicle of the French Revolution.* Schama describes the scene, in part, by quoting from a memoir by Louis-Sébastien Mercier:

> His blood flowed and cries of joy from eighty thousand armed men struck my ears . . . I saw the schoolboys of the Quatre-Nations throw their hats in the air; his blood flowed and some dipped their fingers in it, or a pen or a piece of paper; one tasted it and said *Il est bougrement salé* . . .

You may wish to use this colorful quotation in your own work, but unless you have access to a very large university library, you may have difficulty tracking down the original source. You are still welcome to use the quotation if you attribute the quotation in a citation that follows this format:

27. Louis-Sébastien Mercier, as cited in Simon Schama, *Citizens: A Chronicle of the French Revolution* (New York: Knopf, 1989), 670.

14. Discursive Notes. When you read works of history, you will notice that some authors use endnotes or footnotes to introduce and clarify points of interpretation, or even to take digressions from their subjects. These discursive notes may be fine from the author's point of view, but readers often find them annoying. If something is important enough to say, why not say it in the main body of the text? Discursive footnotes should be restricted to comments about difficulties readers might have in locating or interpreting source materials.

15. Know the Difference Between Note Format and Bibliographic Format. Sometimes you will need to add a bibliography to an essay, especially if it is a long one. Here is a bibliographic format appropriate for books: the author's last name comes first because bibliographies are alphabetized, a period comes after the author's name and after the title, and there are no parentheses around the publication information. With articles, add the full number of pages after the final colon. Bibliographies also usually have a hanging indent, meaning that the first line of an entry is five spaces to the left of the following lines:

Esherick, Joseph W. *Reform and Revolution in China: The 1911 Revolution in Hunan and Hubei.* Berkeley and Los Angeles: University of California Press, 1976.
Harrell, Steven. "Ethnicity, Local Interests, and the State: Yi Communities in Southwest China." *Comparative Studies in Society and History* 32, no. 3 (July 1990): 515–48.

For further questions about bibliographies and citations, see either Turabian or the *Chicago Manual.* These are the authoritative guides for historians.

In addition to covering footnotes and endnotes, two more guides bear mentioning that also offer advice on alternative styles of citation used less frequently in research-based historical essays: the Modern Language Association (MLA) style of in-text citation, commonly used in literature; and the American Psychological Association (APA) style of in-text citation, commonly used in the social sciences.

✍ REVIEW ✍

1. Record and report your sources with care.
2. When you paraphrase or summarize someone else's argument, make it clear.
3. Use the appropriate citation system.
4. Don't forget the bibliography.

Exercise: How to Cite

Add the correct punctuation for Chicago style citations. In each example is a format for (a) a footnote/endnote, (b) a footnote/endnote for the second and subsequent usage, and (c) a bibliography. You can refer to 3I for citing examples and explanations. See page 137–38 for answers.

1. Single-author book citation (refer to 3I.2):

 a. Norman F. Cantor *The Last Knight: The Twilight of the Middle Ages and the Birth of the Modern Era* New York Free Press 2004 24

 b. Cantor *The Last Knight* 25

 c. Cantor Norman F. *The Last Knight: The Twilight of the Middle Ages and the Birth of the Modern Era* New York Free Press 2004

2. Multiauthor book citation (refer to 3I.3):

    a. Jane Burbank and Frederick Cooper *Empires in World History: Power and the Politics of Difference* Princeton Princeton University Press 2010 24–25

    b. Burbank and Cooper *Empires in World History* 26

    c. Burbank Jane and Frederick Cooper *Empires in World History: Power and the Politics of Difference* Princeton Princeton University Press 2010

3. Scholarly article citation (refer to 3I.4):

    a. William G. Rosenberg Reading Soldiers' Moods: Russian Military Censorship and the Configuration of Feeling in World War I *American Historical Review* 119 no. 3 June 2014 715

    b. Rosenberg Reading Soldiers' Moods 720

    c. Rosenberg William G. Reading Soldiers' Moods: Russian Military Censorship and the Configuration of Feeling in World War I *American Historical Review* 119 no. 3 June 2014 714–40

4. Website citation (refer to 3I.6):

    a. Clive Emsley Tim Hitchcock and Robert Shoemaker Gender in the Proceedings *Old Bailey Proceedings Online* www.old-baileyonline.org version 6.0 accessed April 13, 2011

    b. Emsley Hitchcock and Shoemaker Gender in the Proceedings

    c. Emsley Clive Tim Hitchcock and Robert Shoemaker Gender in the Proceedings *Old Bailey Proceedings* Online www.old-baileyonline.org version 6.0 accessed April 13, 2011

4

Using Sources to Make Inferences

It is impossible to know exactly what happened in the past, but this has not stopped people from writing about it. Walt Whitman wrote in *Specimen Days* that the "interior history" of the U.S. Civil War "will not only never be written—its practicality, minutiae of deeds and passions, will never be even suggested."[1] That may be so, but Whitman still tried to interpret the Civil War. He did so by making reasoned inferences.

An inference is more than just a hunch. It is an intelligent conclusion based on examination and comparison of evidence. When Whitman examined the wounded soldiers in a Washington, D.C., army hospital, he concluded that the Civil War was indescribably brutal. Whitman wrote this about the war, and people believed him, even though the poet had not seen every casualty and every battlefield. He had seen enough wounded men to build his inference into a persuasive argument. Like Whitman, historians also suggest probable interpretations by using their sources to make inferences.

What is it, then, that makes an inferential argument interesting? Good writers make inferences by juxtaposing sources in a new, provocative way. Whitman recognized that during the Civil War not everyone wanted to hear a message from a pacifist. People on both sides were mobilizing armies to kill and maim each other, without fully considering the evidence that Whitman saw in the army hospital. Whitman hoped his evidence, built by inferences into an argument, might change the way people thought about the war. New evidence, or a new approach to old evidence, called into question the received wisdom of the day.

Inferential reasoning is based on thoughtful comparison. When modern-day historians write about the past, they assess source materials by cross-checking information. Historians never read sources alone. Even when they have just one source on a given subject, they will read it in the context of their own general knowledge, and they will try as hard as they can to compare a source with other works.

 Be True to Recognized Facts

All inferences begin with a consideration of the facts. Some facts are easy to recognize, but occasionally you may encounter people who are unduly skeptical about recognized facts. Some polemicists posing as historians make extravagant claims about facts. Millions of people witnessed, documented, and experienced the Holocaust, but there is an organization that denies the Holocaust ever happened. It even has its own journal dedicated to "proving" its point.[2] Real historical writers probe factual uncertainties, but they do not invent convenient facts and they do not ignore inconvenient facts.

Transform Facts into Evidence

Facts do not just exist by themselves and conveniently prove things. Historical writers do not just collect facts; they make inferences from them. There is more to writing history than simply gathering facts like the detectives on *Dragnet*. ("Just the facts, ma'am, just the facts.") Even in crime dramas, facts are examined and interpreted in the courtroom. Like "expert witnesses," historians determine the authenticity of factual information. They select only the most reliable and informative facts, and they use only these to make inferences.

Check Your Facts

Sometimes the facts are not what they seem, and it is not always easy to discern where "the facts" stop and interpretation starts. At the end of the 1960s many professional historians believed European ships delivered at least 15 million African slaves to the New World. How did these figures become a fact? Philip Curtin suspected the figure was erroneous. He checked a chain of misguided citations and discovered that the figure of 15 million rested on the speculations of an obscure American pamphleteer who wrote during the 1850s. Curtin inferred from these miscalculations that it would be useful for a modern-day historian to count the number of slaves anew. He conducted his own research, which he published in *The Atlantic Slave Trade: A Census*. In this book, Curtin estimated that 9.5 million slaves were disembarked in the New World.[3] Since Curtin's research in the 1960s, scholars have followed up with more research. Today, the Slave Trade Database at Emory University estimates that 10.7 million slaves arrived in the New World. Historians should follow Curtin's example and take an informed but pragmatic approach to facts. Most often facts will be self-evident, but sometimes historians find that facts rest on nothing more than received wisdom. Historical writers must check their sources. Be aware of the processes for establishing things as factual.

4D Check the Internal Consistency of Primary Sources

A document will not often contradict itself, but if it does, there might be a reason. For example, the richest sources for rural north China in the early twentieth century are the written reports of the Japanese government's South Manchurian Railway Company from 1940 to 1942. These reports contain many contradictions, and for a good reason: during the Japanese occupation, the company sent teams of sociologists to interview large numbers of villagers. Not surprisingly, the peasants of occupied China mistrusted the occupiers, and some-times they lied to them. Even so, several historians have used the interviews as sources to reconstruct the economy, society, and polit-ics of the region.[4] Historians have done this through the use of internal inferences, in other words, by comparing discrete parts of the sources with each other. Individual peasants may have lied to the Japanese on specific issues, meaning all their statements must be checked against each other. These records can still reveal a great deal when used skeptically and responsibly, but historians have not stopped there: they have used them in light of other sources about rural north China, too. All sources are subject to some bias in creation and selection, but this does not mean that historians cannot try to determine what happened.

4E Check Primary Sources Against Each Other

Comparing source materials can lead to important new inferences. To illustrate such a breakthrough inference, it is instructive to examine the well-known life of Louis Pasteur, who made some of the most significant contributions to nineteenth-century biology. After Pasteur died in 1895, his colleagues, admirers, and relatives published chronicles of his life. Historians used these sources skeptically, but they had few alternative accounts that were critical of Pasteur. One of the only critical accounts was written by Pasteur's nephew and laboratory assistant, Adrien Loir. He intimated that at the public trials of the anthrax vaccine, Pasteur misled the judges. However, Loir presented little evidence to support his claim, so most historians continued to trust the positive accounts of Pasteur's supporters. Gerald Geison was the first historian to gain access to Pasteur's laboratory notebooks. When he read them, he found they confirmed Loir's account. Geison then used the notebooks to reevaluate Pasteur's experimental practices, leading him to move Loir's account from the background to the foreground. A simple comparison of sources made it possible to make a significant inference about Pasteur, which provided Geison with a motive to write a book, *The Private Science of Louis Pasteur.*[5] Such source comparisons are at the heart of historical writing.

4F Compare Primary Sources with Secondary Works

Historical knowledge changes incrementally as new interpretations of primary sources alter historians' understanding of the past. Historians often find themselves using primary sources to refine or contradict the ideas other historians present in secondary works. One example comes from the field of environmental history. In Guinea in West Africa, numerous patches of forest can be seen in the grasslands surrounding Kissidougou. From the 1890s until the 1990s, European scientists visited the area. They believed it was a fact that the local inhabitants were converting forest to grassland; the patches of trees were obviously remnants of old forests. They wrote up their opinions in secondary works about the forests. It was only in the 1990s that two outside historians, James Fairhead and Melissa Leach, took the trouble to interview the local people and ask them to explain the patches of trees. They learned some surprising information: for all these years, the villagers had been planting the forest patches in the grasslands. The European scientists had been reading the history of the landscape backwards. The interviews were a primary source that forced a fundamental reconsideration of the secondary works. In their book *Misreading the African Landscape*, Fairhead and Leach showed what every good historical writer knows: historians must cast a skeptical eye on their sources.[6]

4G

Fairhead and Leach uncovered a primary source that called into question a secondary work. The reverse is possible, too. Historian Jan Vansina used a familiar body of secondary works to find a way to look at some new and unfamiliar primary sources. In 1953, Vansina was visiting the Congo for the first time. He had been studying medieval European history, and he had even written his master's thesis on Latin funerary dirges. He knew a lot about the historical literature on medieval Europe, but very little about African history, a subject that few Europeans studied in those days. Vansina met a Kuba village historian named Mbop Louis, who told him, "We too know the past, because we carry our newspapers in our heads." Mbop recited a historical poem, which Vansina thought resembled one of the Latin dirges he knew so well. He used his knowledge of historical methods to formulate an approach to this oral primary source.[7] Vansina went on to write some of the pioneering works in African history, on the basis of his insight that all sources could be compared, no matter how unusual the comparison might be.

4G Conduct Interviews Systematically

Interviewing people can be one of the most exciting aspects of historical research. When you are working on a history, an interview can bring a sense of immediacy to the research and the writing. But an interview is more than just a conversation: it is a way to seek critical information about the past. Be as systematic as possible in your interviewing. Here are some guidelines.

1. Do Your Homework. Before you conduct the interview, learn what you can from written sources. Then make a list of questions that you want to ask your subject. If you do not know some basic information about your history, you will waste your time and your subject's. Your subject will also think you do not know what you are talking about and will not trust you.

2. Be Considerate. Tell your subjects about your project and ask for permission to quote. They may only be willing to share information with you anonymously. You must respect their wishes because their position may be more delicate than you think. If you are a student, your university may also have published ethical guidelines for conducting research with other people as subjects. There may even be laws about "human subjects" in your jurisdiction. Ask your instructor if this is the case, and be sure to follow the guidelines. If you are a graduate student, a postdoctoral researcher, or a faculty member, you will almost certainly be obliged to follow your university's standards for research on human subjects. Detailed advice about interviewing can be found in the third edition of Donald Ritchie's excellent book *Doing Oral History: A Practical Guide* (New York: Oxford University Press, 2014). Another excellent resource may be found online at the website of the Oral History Association. (Go to http://www.oralhistory.org and click on "Resources.") All warnings aside, you will find that many people enjoy being interviewed for a history; it can be very flattering to know that one's experiences have been historically significant.

3. Be Patient. It takes time to interview people, and it may even be difficult to get in touch with some subjects. Often you will find it is a good idea to have references, or even to mail your potential subject a résumé and a brief description of your project. It might also take two or three interviews before your subject trusts you enough to share interesting information with you. If you plan to interview people, start work early so that you can meet your deadlines.

4. Take Scrupulous Notes. Always take written notes during an interview. You may also want to use a digital recorder or smartphone app, but batteries can die and the wrong buttons can get pressed. Back up your work with written notes. Technical problems happen, but they are not the only problems with recorded notes. A recording gives you a more accurate record of the interview, but use of a recorder can also frighten your subjects. If you notice that the recording device is interfering with the interview, shut it off and take notes.

5. Think Critically About Oral Sources. Interviews are often reliable, but they should be subject to critical evaluation. Be aware that your subjects may not remember events exactly as they happened. If it is possible, compare their stories with the stories that other people tell you, and also compare oral sources with any available written sources. Written sources are not necessarily more reliable than oral sources, but writing can often be a more effective way to preserve a version of history.

6. Cultivate Your Skills as an Interviewer and as an Interpreter of Interviews. It takes a lot of practice to learn how to work with sources, and interviewing is no different. The best interviewers are usually the most experienced. There are also a number of good guides to interviewing. For a formal introduction, see Donald Ritchie's book, mentioned earlier, as well as the "Smithsonian Folklife and Oral History Guide."

4H Compare Sources to Make Inferences

During the course of your research and writing, you will be constantly reading sources in the context of other sources. You will need to check primary sources and secondary works for internal consistency. You will also need to compare primary sources and secondary works against each other. How might all this advice work together in practice?

Imagine you are beginning with a primary source, a song by Robert Johnson, from the Mississippi Delta, called "Crossroads Blues," recorded in the 1930s:

I went down to the crossroads,
Fell down on my knees.

I went down to the crossroads,
Fell down on my knees.
Ask the lord above for mercy,
Say boy, if you please.

What can historians tell from only the text of this song? The singer goes to the crossroads to pray, and even as he asks God for mercy, he employs a somewhat irreverent tone. Historians know that Johnson sang it in the Delta, but the song itself does not seem to make any particular reference to the place. Standing by itself, this song may not be very interesting, at least from a historical standpoint.

Perhaps the "Crossroads Blues" only refers to praying, but historians might be able to gain a better understanding of the song if they knew something about Robert Johnson. In a book called *Standing at the Crossroads*, historian Pete Daniel writes that as a young man Johnson knew the blues artists Son House, Willie Brown, and Charley Patton. During the 1920s, all of them worked and played in the vicinity of the Dockery plantation in the Mississippi Delta. Johnson could not play as well as the others, and at one point he simply disappeared, seemingly leaving for good. But several months later Johnson reappeared, having become a much better guitar player. The legend developed that Johnson had gone down to the crossroads and sold his soul to the Devil so he could play the blues. This legend casts some light on how Johnson's audience understood the song.[8] Historians might reasonably make the inference that Johnson played the song to perpetuate a legend among his audience.

Pete Daniel makes it possible to interpret the "Crossroads Blues" in the context of the legends surrounding Johnson's life, but it might be possible to make further inferences about the song from some other comparisons. The references to the Devil are fascinating, and it might be possible to find a source that would place Johnson's song in the context of African American religious practices. In a history of the Delta called *The Most Southern Place on Earth*, James Cobb argues that blues musicians, like other African Americans, had a different concept of the Devil from European Americans. The Devil was not a sinister Satan but a playful trickster who resembled the African god

Legba. When Johnson associated himself with the Devil, he was advertising himself as dangerous, but not as European Americans might conventionally understand it.[9]

Is there any validity to this position? Could Robert Johnson's song have anything to do with African religious practices that were retained in African American culture? Tracing a few footnotes makes it possible to draw further inferences from textual comparisons. Several essays in a collection edited by Joseph Holloway, *Africanisms in American Culture*, substantiate the case that African religious and musical practices were indeed retained and developed in African American culture. One essay by Robert Farris Thompson shows plenty of evidence to suggest that crosses and crossroads were considered to be sacred by the Kongo people, and these symbols remained important in African American art and folklore. Another essay, by Margaret Washington Creel, tells more about the significance of the cross in Kongo religious practices. Archaeological evidence and oral histories suggest that the cross was a symbol in Kongo religion long before the introduction of Christianity to the region, and that during the Christian era Kongo ideas about religion can be found in coastal Georgia and South Carolina.[10] When read in the context of this information, Robert Johnson's song becomes a significant piece of evidence for building the case that some elements of African culture survived the experience of slavery.

Creel supports her argument partly by making reference to John Janzen and Wyatt MacGaffey, who published a collection of Kongo oral histories during the 1970s. One of MacGaffey's recorded texts is particularly interesting to compare with the "Crossroads Blues." In it, a man named Kingani describes how he went to the crossroads and prayed to the spirits of his ancestors for the health of his child.[11] This Kongo text bears an obvious resemblance to Robert Johnson's song. Such a comparison does not show that Johnson was necessarily conscious of African religious traditions. It does suggest the inference that Johnson may have been drawing on a folk tradition having its origins on the other side of the Atlantic. Making such inferences by comparisons can make it easier to appreciate any discrete piece of evidence.

Make Inferences About Visual and Material Sources

Most academic writers analyze written sources. Therefore, it takes some practice for historians to learn how to approach images and objects as sources. But many historians, including historians of science and technology, archaeologists, and art historians, do work frequently with objects. Learning to analyze objects can give you new perspectives on things, but it is not easy to learn how. Try to follow these guidelines, which are borrowed from an article by Jules Prown called "Mind in Matter." These are common methods used by writers across the disciplines to analyze images and materials.

1. Describing the Image or Object. What can you observe in the source itself? Give a physical description of the object, or of the image and the things that are portrayed. How is it shaped? If you can measure it, what are its dimensions (size, weight)? If you cannot measure it, estimate the dimensions. Can you find any obvious symbols on the object, such as markings, decorations, or inscriptions?

2. Thinking About the Object. In the case of objects, what is it like to interact with the object? What does the object feel like? When you use the object, do you have to take into account its size, weight, or shape? What does the object do, and how does it do it? Does it work well? What is it like to use it? How do you feel about using this object? Do you like it? Does it frustrate you? Is it puzzling? In the case of an image, how does it compare to other images? Does it have patterns and shapes that are similar to or different from other images? Does it contain recognizable styles?

3. Making an Argument About the Image or Object. Can you analyze this source imaginatively and plausibly? Review your descriptions and deductions. What sorts of hypotheses can you make? Can you make a historically significant argument about the object or the image? What might it have been like for someone to use this object in the past, or to see this image? Use other sources as a lens for interpreting the object. What other evidence can you use to test your hypotheses, speculations, and deductions?[12]

4J Move from Inferences to Arguments

The process of making inferences allows historians to say something new. This can be an intimidating proposition, especially if you are working on a topic that has been studied extensively. But judging by the contents of most bookstores, I would say historians are always finding something new to say about old topics. Just when you think the Second World War has been studied to death, a new book appears.

There are many ways to say something new. Experienced historians know that new ideas come out of close and careful comparisons of primary sources and secondary works. A new idea in one field can shed light on an old source; the discovery of a new source can inspire historians to rethink some old ideas. In fact, every individual historian brings a unique personal perspective to all sources.

Still, novelty is not enough. Small inferences must be built into larger arguments, and arguments must be made persuasively. When you read your sources, start thinking about ways to compose your essay. How can you move from asking questions about events and sources to composing a story and an argument of your own? This is the most challenging aspect to writing any history. You must consider the arguments of your primary sources and secondary works, and then engage them constructively and responsibly.

4K Make Reasonable Inferences from Your Sources

Source materials impose healthy constraints on historical writers. You may have a hunch that space aliens helped the Egyptians build the pyramids, but after careful review of primary sources and secondary works, you will find no evidence to support your hypothesis. Don't worry. You thought you could make a breathtakingly new argument, but it is much more important that you recognize the limits of your sources. Do not expect too much from your sources, and do not read into them what you hope to find. You can even write an essay about how little you can tell sometimes from the sources. Even so, if you cannot use a source to support your argument, you must be prepared to either redefine your questions or move on to another set of sources.

4L Make Inferences That Are Warranted

Some inferences are better than others, but how do historians know what makes a good inference? Historians must have a reason to believe an inference. Hence, it is important to try to answer the question, Under which circumstances are inferences warranted?

The ancient Greeks divided arguments from inferences into two categories: deduction and induction. When you are reading and writing history, use the categories of deduction and induction to help you decide which arguments from inferences are warranted.

1. Deductive Reasoning. In deductive reasoning, a writer makes an inference based on a limited amount of evidence, but the inference is still trustworthy because it is consonant with conventional wisdom. In other words, deduction means that we are applying general rules to particular circumstances.

Writers understand deductions by breaking deductive warrants down into their stated and unstated components. Here is an example of a historical deduction: "The gaps in the Watergate tapes must mean that Nixon was trying to hide something." What sort of evidence do historians have to support this statement? The Watergate tapes do contain large gaps, but Nixon never admitted to hiding anything; he said his secretary accidentally erased portions of the tapes. Why didn't anybody believe Nixon? Common sense indicates that Nixon erased key, incriminating passages from the tapes. Most people would argue that Nixon had a motive, and he also had access.

If you break the argument down into its deductive components, this is what it looks like:

- Evidence: the Watergate tapes contain large gaps.
- Commonsense warrant: people erase tapes to destroy information.
- Inference: when Nixon delivered the incomplete Watergate tapes to investigators, he must have been hiding something.

Usually writers do not state their reasoning so schematically, but a commonsense deduction can provide a warrant for believing an inference based on a limited source.

In some cases common sense is obvious, but sometimes it is deceptive. It is possible to challenge the inferences of historical writers by testing whether their warrants really are based on common sense. All historians have heard the story about how Columbus wanted to prove that the earth was round and not flat. According to the legend, Columbus's contemporaries believed the earth was flat because they had a weak commonsense warrant:

- Evidence: the earth appears to be flat.
- Commonsense warrant: people can distinguish between flat objects and round objects.
- Inference: the earth is flat, not round.

Obviously, people may not actually be able to distinguish flat objects from round objects, at least not on the planetary scale. If your commonsense warrant does not make sense, then there must be a flaw in your reasoning. Take care to test your warrants, especially if they are unstated. If you don't test your own warrants, your audience surely will.

2. Inductive Reasoning. Historians commonly associate inductive reasoning with scientific methods. This is because inductive reasoning begins with many particular bits of evidence and generalizes from them. During your reading and research you may observe many facts, perceive relationships between them, and draw conclusions about them.

Induction operates on the warrant that plenty of data can help historians reach likely conclusions. Take this statement: "Census reports indicate that between 1890 and 1990 American life spans increased significantly." What are the components of this inductive statement?

- Evidence: Census reports from 1890 to 1990 show that Americans died at increasingly older ages.
- Inductive warrant: plenty of data help people to reach likely conclusions.
- Inference: on the basis of the evidence, we could say American life spans increased significantly.

The most common way to test such an inference is to question whether the evidence is sufficient. The underlying inductive warrant is difficult to challenge.

4M Avoid Unwarranted Comparisons

Comparisons lie at the heart of historical reasoning, so be careful when you make them. Some comparisons help historians make strong inferences about the past; other comparisons are pointless or even irresponsible. In a book called *The Unmasterable Past*, Charles Maier writes about how German historians have interpreted Nazism and the Holocaust. While surveying his topic, Maier makes the point that some historical comparisons are "licit" and some are not. The Holocaust will probably always be understood in the context of other genocides and acts of brutality, but Maier criticizes those historians who compare the Holocaust to other genocides so as to alleviate German guilt.[13] Historians must use comparisons to build inferences that are appropriate.

4N Avoid Anachronistic Inferences

When historians write history they speak on behalf of people who lived in the past. This is a tremendous responsibility and challenge, which is why anachronistic interpretations have no place in historical writing. Historians can bring latter-day interpretations to bear on their subjects, but they cannot place their subjects in situations they would never recognize.

Some anachronisms are easy to avoid. No sensible person would ever write this sentence: "Just before Caesar crossed the Rubicon, he glanced at his wristwatch and wondered if it would ever be time for tea." Obviously, Caesar did not have a wristwatch or tea. Even so, anachronisms often present subtler problems. For example, historian Georges Lefebvre wanted to use Marxist theory to explain the origins of the French Revolution. But when Lefebvre wrote the book *The Coming of the French Revolution*, he knew he could not argue that the French working classes intended to form a communist party and establish a dictatorship of the proletariat. Such an anachronistic claim would not have been true to the experience of eighteenth-century French people, who had never heard of such things as the communist party or the dictatorship of the proletariat. Instead, Lefebvre gained a heightened awareness of class conflict from reading Marx, and then used this awareness to ask new questions of his sources.[14]

Many students get interested in history because they want to explain the origins of contemporary problems. This is a common way to ask questions about the past, but historians must also respect the outlook of people who lived in the past. For example, historians may see the origins of modern physics in Newton's *Principia*, but Newton must be understood in the context of the seventeenth century. Like many of his contemporaries, he had interests in alchemy and religion that bear little relation to modern physics and that may seem bizarre and even foolish from a modern perspective. As Betty Jo Teeter Dobbs shows in her book *The Janus Face of Genius*, it is important for a historian to understand Newton's own perspective and to ask how his understanding of mechanics related to his understanding of alchemy and religion.[15] The power of hindsight makes it perfectly legitimate for historical writers to ask contemporary questions about old materials, but historians must remain faithful to the perspective of the people who lived through the times under study.

∽ REVIEW ∾

1. Think! What does your evidence tell you?
2. Think! What does your evidence not tell you?
3. Check facts carefully.
4. Compare evidence from a variety of sources.
5. Develop an argument based on all the evidence.
6. Be true to your characters' reality.

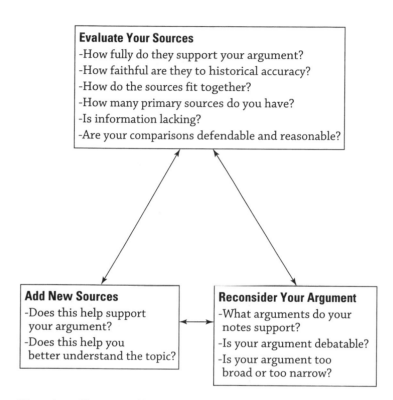

Evaluate Your Sources
-How fully do they support your argument?
-How faithful are they to historical accuracy?
-How do the sources fit together?
-How many primary sources do you have?
-Is information lacking?
-Are your comparisons defendable and reasonable?

Add New Sources
-Does this help support
your argument?
-Does this help you
better understand the topic?

Reconsider Your Argument
-What arguments do your
notes support?
-Is your argument debatable?
-Is your argument too
broad or too narrow?

Flowchart Chapter 4 Understanding Sources

5 Get Writing! Get Organized

After spending days, weeks, or months gathering and analyzing information, the time will come when you have to make the transition from research to writing. This is often the most difficult stage of a project, but it must be done. Scholars facing the blank computer screen would do well to heed the advice of Samuel Eliot Morison, one of the greatest historians of the mid-twentieth century. In an article called "History as a Literary Art: An Appeal to Young Historians," Morison advised students to avoid the temptation to find that one last source or to brew another pot of coffee. Instead of procrastinating, Morison insisted that his students should "First and foremost, *get writing!*"[1] Once you start to write, you will have to think more rigorously about what it is that you want to say.

5A Craft a Thesis Statement

By now, your hypothesis is beginning to take the form of a thesis statement. A thesis statement is usually one sentence summarizing the main ideas of your argument. It guides the readers through the essay. In short analytical essays written by students, the thesis statement is often placed near the end of an introductory paragraph. In a longer, research-based essay, the thesis statement is often articulated after several paragraphs have introduced the underlying motive for the research by reviewing the main secondary works in the field. In either case, a simple test may be applied to see whether a thesis statement is workable. Its purpose is to summarize the argument, so test to see if it is a good argument. Read the statement out loud and ask yourself:

1. Is this thesis statement a claim that can actually be argued about, or would most reasonable people agree or disagree?
2. Will it be possible to support the thesis by reference to recognized evidence?

If the answers to these questions are "yes," write the thesis statement at the top of a blank page. You are ready to fill the rest of the page with your outline.

5B Create a Draft Outline of an Analytical Essay

By now you will also know which pieces of evidence you will be using to support your main argument. But chances are you do not know yet whether you will organize the essay as one long narrative touching on analytical topics, or as an analysis using short narratives to illustrate specific points. In the early stages of writing, it is usually a good idea to make an outline of your essay. Here you will merely sketch out the broader organization of an essay to test its feasibility.

If you are still writing a paper on colonial U.S. environmental history that focuses on William Bartram, a draft outline of an analytical essay might look something like this:

I. Introduction: science, nature, and exploration in colonial America
II. William Bartram
   A. His early years
   B. His travels in the Southeast U.S.
   C. Later years
III. Bartram's principal contributions
   A. Botany
   B. Birds and animals
   C. Ethnography

    IV. Conclusion

        A. How others appreciated Bartram

        B. Significance of his life

This is an analytical essay because it is organized around Bartram. It does not tell one narrative, but it contains several narratives: the story of Bartram, the stories of how Bartram learned about different aspects of the Southeast, and the story of how others appreciated him.

5C Create a Draft Outline of a Narrative Essay

It is also possible to organize your essay around one narrative. In this case, you may have enough information about Bartram to use his life's story as a narrative that contains within it important analytical points. Here is a possible draft outline of a narrative essay:

    I. Bartram's youth

        A. Education and training, under his father's supervision

        B. Becomes aware of scientific problems and methods

    II. Bartram's travels

        A. Scientific findings in Carolinas

        B. Scientific findings in Georgia

        C. Scientific findings in Florida

        D. Scientific findings in Alabama

    III. Bartram at the end of his life

        A. Acclaim for his work

        B. Bartram's death and legacy for science and history

5D Complete Your Outline

Now that you have explored how to organize your essay around analysis and narrative, it is time to choose the right framework. You must think about several questions. Which framework is best suited to your sources? Which framework will be most enjoyable to use? Which framework does your audience expect?

    The preceding draft outlines offer only skeletal frameworks for either an analytical essay or a narrative essay. They may be useful as a beginning, but they do not do much to help you articulate your argument. If you want a complete outline of your analytical essay, add some flesh to the bones. A complete outline of an essay would explain why you are moving from one section to another.

5E Start to Write a First Draft

The complete outlines given earlier contain frameworks for sustained arguments. A good outline shows the main argument as well as its significance, and it shows how subsequent sections of the argument are related to the main argument. And yet it does not really prove anything. It is, after all, only an outline.

As you think about the overall outline, go to the sources, find support for your possible arguments, and compose paragraphs around them. It is fine to start composing paragraphs that will fall in the middle of the essay, not in the beginning. An introduction does not have to be written first; indeed, you may wish to write the body of the text first. As you grapple with writing about your sources, you will discover new things about them, things that will make an early version of the introduction obsolete by the time you finish the body of the text.

It is not enough that a historical essay should have an introduction, a series of paragraphs with evidence, and a conclusion. A good historical essay leads its readers in some direction, but it should also be said that it is challenging for a writer to articulate and sustain this direction. This is why it is crucial for an essay to have an argument. An argument is not an angry display of vituperation; it is an idea that develops over the course of an essay. An argument must capture and hold an audience's attention.

While you are writing a first draft, keep your argument in mind and think about how it is evolving. As you add more analysis and information, stand back occasionally to check and see whether your argument is developing reasonably and interestingly. You may even find yourself changing your line of argument to the point where it does not even resemble your original argument any more. If this is so, you must return to the beginning and check the entire argument for consistency.

5F Grab Your Reader's Attention, But Do It Gently

Every reader asks, "Why should I read this?" "Why should I care?" A writer must give the audience a reason to care. Many historians use the beginning of an essay or book to connect their scholarly interests to broader academic and political debates. For example, in a book called *Holy Feast and Holy Fast*, which is about medieval religious women, Caroline Walker Bynum begins with a quick discussion of the scholarship in her field. Then she grabs the reader's attention:

> Sex and money . . . again and again modern scholars have emphasized the guilt engendered by their seductiveness, the awesome heroism required for their renunciation. Yet this modern focus may tell us more about the twentieth century than about the late Middle Ages. In our industrialized corner of the globe, where food supplies do not fail, we scarcely notice grain or milk, ever-present supports of life, and yearn rather after money or sexual favors as signs of power and of success.[2]

Notice the tone of Bynum's paragraph. It addresses topics of universal interest like sex, money, and food, but it does so calmly and methodically. You do not need to drop a bomb to get your reader's attention. Be relevant, but be gentle. People prefer to read essays they find agreeable, trustworthy, and authoritative. Even when you suspect your audience may disagree with you, it behooves you to treat them with some moderation. Put them in the right frame of mind to listen to your argument.

5G State Your Intellectual Interests Early

In the preceding example, Bynum caught the reader's attention by appealing to some personal interests. Your readers will also expect you to give them a sense of your intellectual interests. What are the broader historical problems your essay addresses? Why have you chosen your specific topic to explore these interests? What argument will be developing over the course of your essay? Address these questions in the beginning of your essay, or else you will run the risk of confusing and losing your readers.

One introduction that answers these questions comes from an article by Samuel K. Cohn, Jr., about the Black Death. He begins in this way:

> HIV/AIDS and the threat of biological warfare have refueled interest in the Black Death among professional historians, biologists, and the public, not only for assessing the toxic effects of the bacillus but for understanding the psychological and longer-term cultural consequences of mass death. This article makes two arguments. Against the assumptions of historians and scientists for over a century and what continues to be inscribed in medical and history texts alike, the Black Death was not the same disease as that rat-based bubonic plague whose agent (*Yersinia pestis*) was first cultured at Hong Kong in 1894. The two diseases were radically different in their signs, symptoms, and epidemiologies. The proof of these differences forms the major thrust of this article. The second argument stems from the epidemiological differences between the two diseases. Humans have no natural immunity to modern bubonic plague, whereas populations of Western Europe adapted rapidly to the pathogen of the Black Death for at least the first hundred years. The success of their immune systems conditioned a cultural response that departs from the common wisdom about "plagues and peoples." As far back as Thucydides, historians have seen the aftershocks of pestilence as raising the level of violence, tearing asunder secular cultures, and spawning pessimism and transcendental religiosities. A fresh reading of the late medieval sources across intellectual strata from merchant chronicles to the plague tracts of university-trained doctors shows another trajectory, an about-face in the reactions to the plague after its initial onslaught. This change in spirit casts new light on the Renaissance, helping to explain why a new emphasis on "fame and glory" should have arisen in the wake of the West's most monumental mortality.[3]

In this introduction, Cohn captures the reader's interest by mentioning present-day fears of epidemic diseases and biological weapons.

Then he quickly introduces two related arguments that will interest anyone who has ever read about the Black Death. The first is that the Black Death may not have been caused by bubonic plague, for which there is no immunity. The second is that Europeans appear to have gradually developed immunity to the pathogen that caused Black Death, and this immunological success may have inspired people, rather than disheartening them.

Cohn's arguments are radical. He presents them as "paradigm shifts" that overturn a century of scholarship on the Black Death. Cohn highlights the originality of his argument, yet he establishes a reasoned tone that will cause even the most skeptical historians to consider his arguments carefully. He does not write scathingly about previous historians. Instead, he uses an excellent strategy. He starts to build his case in the first paragraph by giving us a glimpse of the evidence he has considered: "late medieval sources" ranging from "merchant chronicles to the plague tracts of university-trained doctors."

5G
When an audience begins to read Cohn's article, they know why they should be interested; they know which problems the author is addressing; and they have some idea of how the author will approach these problems. In the first paragraph of this article, the author has given his audience much to anticipate.

The example from Cohn's article shows that an argument—and a related argument—may be made in the opening of an essay. It is more typical for an essay to make one argument, a claim that may be argued about on the basis of evidence. Usually historian-authors state the argument clearly and concisely near the opening of the essay in what is called the "thesis statement." Some teachers prefer for students to conclude the introductory paragraph with a clear argument. Other teachers (and many professional writers) allow for some flexibility. Either way, place the thesis statement near the beginning of the essay, so that readers may grasp your argument as early as possible.

Historian Paul Josephson begins his essay "The Ocean's Hot Dog: The Development of the Fish Stick," with a clear thesis statement that I have italicized:

The fish stick—the bane of schoolchildren who generally consider it an overcooked, bread-encrusted, cardboard-tasting, fish-less effort of lunchrooms and mothers to deceive them into consuming protein—is a postwar invention that came into existence as the confluence of several forces of modernity. These forces included a boom in housing construction that contained kitchens with such new appliances as freezers, the seeming appeal of space-age ready-to-eat foods, the rise of consumer culture; and an increasingly affluent society. *Yet the fish stick arose during the 1950s not because consumers cried out for it and certainly not because school children demanded it but because of the need to process and sell tons of fish that were harvested from the ocean, filleted, and frozen in huge, solid blocks.* Consumers were not attracted by the form of these frozen fillets, however, and demand for fish products remained low. Manufacturers believed that the fish stick—a breaded, precooked food—would solve the problem. Still, several simultaneous technological advances had to take place before the product could appear.[4]

5H

The first sentence catches our attention and then situates the seemingly banal fish stick in a serious discussion. The thesis statement tells us that the developers of the fish stick did not sense a strong demand. On the contrary, they had an oversupply of frozen fish and needed to get rid of it! Supply, rather than demand, can drive the history of innovation.

5H Review the Historical Literature

All historians know that reading deeply and widely helps us become better analysts. Historical writers build common ground with their audience by demonstrating knowledge of their topic's historical context. Historical essays often start with a review of the historical writing in one or more fields of history. In an essay entitled "Putting the Ocean in Atlantic History," Jeffrey Bolster begins by writing that most historians of the Atlantic world have overlooked the history of the ocean itself. To demonstrate that he knows Atlantic history well enough to make such a claim, he summarizes the field in general terms, writing that it is "known for blurring historiographical and disciplinary boundaries, ignoring national boundaries, and probing novel social and cultural interactions," adding a footnote that references a dozen key recent works. He compares Atlantic history to the history of other oceanic regions, stating that "proliferating histories of oceans and seas are reorienting conventional geographies and emphasizing oceans as access points for innovative regional histories." Another footnote references another dozen sources. Bolster then reviews those historians who have written about the political and economic history of the Atlantic, with a footnote to half a dozen sources. Bolster praises historians, journalists, and ecologists who are working together to understand changes to marine ecologies, with eight references to their work. He concludes that most historians slight the role of nature in the modern Atlantic world, and then he cites the work of seven historians who do successfully incorporate nature. Further references are made to environmental historians who do or do not engage with the history of the oceans. This scholar leaves no doubt in anybody's mind that he has done the kind of background reading that is essential to his ultimate argument: that between 1500 and 1800 New Englanders transformed the Northwest Atlantic, which in turn transformed their own societies.[5] Student writers need not demonstrate the kind of reading that can be done over the course of thirty years. Even so, consider that readers will want any writer to demonstrate familiarity with recognized, authoritative writing about their subject area. Such familiarity indicates to readers that the author will make worthy observations.

5I Build Your Essay with Good Paragraphs

A paragraph is much more than just an indented block of text. Good paragraphs develop inferences from sources, and they also contribute to the overall argument of the essay. To accomplish all this, here is what the best paragraphs do.

1. Make a Transition from the Previous Paragraph. Readers want to know why they are moving from one paragraph to the next. Good paragraphs connect to each other with one or two transition sentences, signposts that remind readers where they have been and also tell them where they are going.

2. State the Argument of the Paragraph. Each paragraph presents and develops an argument that supports the overall development of the essay. Sometimes the argument may be located in the transition or "signpost" sentences; other times you may wish to write a separate "thesis sentence."

3. Present Evidence to Support the Argument of the Paragraph. What sort of evidence do you have to support the argument of this paragraph? Present the information from your sources that has helped you make historical inferences.

In the abstract, these three components of the paragraph sound easy to manage. In fact, it takes discipline and creativity to practice this advice. The best historical writers produce paragraphs that blend together a transition, an argument, and evidence, but there are many ways to do this. There is not one common structure for every paragraph.

If you are looking for a model of successful paragraphing, consider Daniel Headrick's history of the global spread of European technologies, *The Tools of Empire*. In the fourth chapter, Headrick discusses how firearms changed during the nineteenth century:

> At the beginning of the nineteenth century the standard weapon of the European infantryman was the muzzle-loading smoothbore musket. It had a flintlock to detonate the powder through a hole in the breech and a bayonet that could be attached to the barrel for hand-to-hand combat. The Brown Bess, which British soldiers used until 1853, was much the same weapon their forefathers had carried at Blenheim in 1704. It had an official range of 200 yards but an effective one of 80, less than that of a good bow. Despite admonitions to

withhold their fire until they saw the whites of their enemies' eyes, soldiers commonly shot away their weight in lead for every man they killed. These muskets took at least a minute to load, so to maintain a steady rate of fire on the battlefield, soldiers were drilled in the countermarch, each rank advancing in turn to shoot, then falling back to reload.

One of the most serious drawbacks of the flintlock muskets was their poor firing record. Under the best conditions, they fired only seven out of ten times, and in rain or damp weather they ceased firing altogether. For this reason soldiers were trained to use their weapons as pikes. In 1807, Alexander Forsyth, a Scottish clergyman and amateur chemist, offered a solution to this problem; using the violent explosive potassium chlorate as a detonating powder and a percussion lock instead of a flintlock, he made a gun that could fire in any weather. Tests showed that a percussion lock musket misfired only 4.5 times per thousand rounds, compared to 411 times for a flintlock. After 1814, Joshua Shaw of Philadelphia improved upon Forsyth's invention by putting the detonating powder into little metal caps, thereby simplifying the loading process and making the weapons even more impervious to the elements.[6]

Notice how Headrick makes the transition from the first to the second paragraph. In the first paragraph, he was discussing some of the drawbacks to the old muzzle-loading muskets. He begins the second paragraph by telling readers that he is now going to discuss one of the most *serious* problems. Readers are still learning from him about problems with muskets, but he is introducing them to a new way to evaluate the muskets. Headrick also presents plenty of evidence (and in the original text, each paragraph ends with a note to his sources). The paragraphs develop intellectually; they are supported by evidence; and they relate closely to the broader argument he is making about the history of firearms. Headrick's paragraphs guide readers by relating the significance of the evidence to his broader point.

5J Define Your Key Terms Early

Do not assume that you and your audience understand important concepts to mean the same thing. Define them as soon as you introduce them, preferably in the beginning of your essay. You will find that you can use a definition as a springboard to discuss the complexities of your subject.

1. Defining Uncommon Terms. Sometimes you will need to define specialized or foreign terms that your audience might not recognize. In his 1995 lecture to the History of Science Society on the subject of Arab science, A. I. Sabra discussed the role of the *muwaqqit*. What or who, you may wonder, is a *muwaqqit*? According to Sabra, it is a timekeeper in a mosque who uses astronomical methods to determine the exact timing of the five daily prayers. But when Sabra defines this term, he takes the opportunity to discuss one of the things that make Arab science distinctive. According to him, "Through the introduction, apparently, for the first time under the Mamluks, of the office of *muwaqqit*, the timekeeper in charge of regulating the times of the five daily prayers, a place was created for the utilization of one form of scientific knowledge in a permanent religious institution." Sabra defines the word in such a way that it causes readers to think of a larger problem: the relations between religion and science.[7]

2. Redefining Common Terms. *Muwaqqit* demands definition, but sometimes you will even need to redefine commonly used English words, such as "landscape." This is exactly what William Cronon does in his book *Changes in the Land*. The *American Heritage Dictionary* defines *landscape* as a "view or vista of scenery on land," but Cronon uses the word more broadly. When he looks at the ecological transformation of colonial New England, he tells a story that relates the management of natural resources to cultural and political debates among the Native Americans and English settlers. Cronon's New Englanders saw that the "landscape was a visible confirmation of the state of human society."[8] An English landscape, a way of viewing and ordering the world, prevailed over a Native American landscape.

5K Set an Appropriate Tone

All historians must build a relationship with their audience. The best way to establish rapport is to find an appropriate, trustworthy tone.

1. Avoid the First Person Singular. Generally speaking, historical writers do not write in the first person singular. Historians all recognize that personal biases enter historical writing; there is usually no need to overemphasize it. A weak historical writer would state, "In my opinion, Frederick Jackson Turner ignored the role of Native Americans in the emergence of democratic institutions." The writer might just as well say, "Frederick Jackson Turner ignored the role of Native Americans in the emergence of democratic institutions," and spare readers the extra verbiage. Readers may confidently infer that this is the writer's opinion.

Usually historians employ the first person singular only when they have personally experienced a phenomenon they are describing. They introduce this personal information to explain their own relationship to the subject matter. For example, Carl Degler begins his book about racial thinking in anthropology, *In Search of Human Nature*, by writing, "Like most white Americans of my sex and class (the son of a fireman) and my generation (born in 1921) I came into a world that soon made me a racist and a sexist."[9] He does this to draw the reader's attention to personal and social issues of bias. He also honestly informs readers that he bears a close personal relationship to his subject, something they may wish to know when they evaluate his arguments.

2. Be Judicious and Dispassionate. All historians pass judgment on their subjects, but don't be too heavy-handed. If your subjects engaged in some particularly horrible activity, it is important to strike a balance between the rendering of judgment and the presentation of evidence. Some of the most difficult evidence to handle comes from

Nazi Germany, and here are two historians who built trustworthy arguments by using a judicious, dispassionate tone.

Psychiatrist and historian Robert Jay Lifton wanted to learn why medical doctors served the Nazi regime. He uses Dr. Josef Mengele as a case in point—a distasteful case indeed. Lifton writes in his book *The Nazi Doctors* that Mengele "committed real crimes, murderous crimes, direct murder ... These crimes included selections, lethal injections, shootings, beatings, and other forms of deliberate killing." All this is well known, but the power of Lifton's work comes from his judicious argumentation. He describes Mengele's "research" matter-of-factly and puts Mengele's experiments in the context of the Nazi's medical career: "More than any other SS doctor, Mengele realized himself in Auschwitz. There he came into his own—found expression for his talents." Mengele remained the consummate clinical researcher, even in the midst of a concentration camp. Lifton presents Mengele objectively and ironically, so that readers will trust the book's conclusion: that Mengele had a schizoid personality, making it easier for him to detach himself from the suffering he inflicted on others.[10]

5K

It is often enough just to describe a horrible activity in a subtle and ironic way. Your readers will understand that you have chosen to describe this activity because you find it repugnant. William Sheridan Allen wanted to learn how the Nazis came to power. Instead of focusing on well-known politicians in Berlin, he wrote a book called *The Nazi Seizure of Power* that focuses on the activities of the Nazi Party (NSDAP) in a small German town called Northeim. He describes how the Nazis used public events to sustain enthusiasm for their cause:

> Then on Sunday, March 19, the Northeim NSDAP gave its victory celebration, fittingly held in the Cattle Auction Hall. The hall, decorated with swastika flags, was full to the bursting point with at least a thousand people. The chief speaker was the Nazi preacher, Pastor Muenchmeyer, and his topic: "What a Transposition Through Divine Disposition!" The whole tone of the celebration was conservative, solemn, and religious.[11]

Allen does not call the Nazis cattle; the Cattle Auction Hall is an appropriate place for their meeting. He does not say that the pastor and his audience are intellectual mediocrities; he gives the title of the speech. Allen makes his point—that the Nazis were dangerous, obsequious drones—cleverly and subtly in a reasoned tone.

5L Treat Other Writers with Consideration

Scholarship is a very fragile enterprise. It thrives on lively debate and open disagreement, but it depends on mutual respect and careful consideration. When you write about other historians, give them the same amount of respect you would give if you were speaking to them in person. Do not oversimplify or misconstrue the arguments of your opponents, and do not make personal attacks on opponents to discredit their arguments.

5M Account for Counterarguments

Do not select one argument and ignore all the other possibilities. When you acknowledge the possibility of alternative interpretations you increase the credibility and complexity of your own work. Your readers will not think you are weak; they will think you are openminded. In fact, your readers may already be aware of some possible contradictions to your argument, and they will expect you to deal with them.

By the very nature of their work, historians know it is impossible to write a flawless interpretation of anything. Knowledge is a slippery thing. In a short essay, it is often effective to note a few main counterarguments toward the end, and then conclude by reasserting why you still wish to articulate your own position. In a longer essay, thesis, or book, authors often engage in multiple counterarguments as they consider the evidence.

One such example of counterargumentation can be found in Robert McElvaine's book *Eve's Seed: Biology, the Sexes, and the Course of History*. McElvaine reviews evidence from prehistory and also from evolutionary psychology that suggests humans are adaptable social animals who are both competitive and cooperative. Their cooperative side inclines them to build families and groups in which both sexes work together. For most of human history, differences between the sexes did not necessarily result in the subordination of one sex to another. McElvaine argues it was the Agricultural Revolution, starting around 10,000 BCE, that caused men to subordinate women in almost every culture. According to McElvaine, men lost their roles as hunters, and then, out of insecurity and envy, they turned to misogyny. Patriarchy in the home mirrored male domination in politics, religion, and business. Male domination is not natural; it can be explained historically.

To make this argument, McElvaine has to address two possible counterarguments: that human behavior is completely determined by biology, and the opposite argument, that all people are born with a clean slate and it is nurture, not nature, that is important.

McElvaine wants to show that nature and nurture are both important. First, he engages these two opposite positions with a joke. Quoting his own father in an early chapter title, he writes that people are "90 percent nature and 90 percent nurture." Next he moves to consider the "nurture" position, espoused by many contemporary American liberals. McElvaine writes:

> The reason that so many liberals have clung to their insistence that human nature should be ignored is, I believe, a fundamental misapprehension concerning the implications of human nature. They have feared that the admission of the existence of innate characteristics will lead to findings on how people *differ*. In fact, the real meaning of human nature, as [Franz] Boas understood, is to be found in showing the ways in which people are *alike*. As Robert Wright has said, unlike the old social Darwinists, "today's Darwinian anthropologists, in scanning the world's peoples, focus less on surface differences among cultures than on deep unities."

After considering the "liberal" position, McElvaine turns to the "conservatives," who often believe in the determining power of genetics over human nature. He quotes from the work of Richard Dawkins and Edward Wilson, two "sociobiologists" who have written that people "are machines created by our genes," and that "human behavior . . . is the circuitous technique by which human genetic material has been and will be kept intact. Morality has no other demonstrable ultimate function." In response to these "biodeterministic" arguments, McElvaine writes:

> As Darwinism had been a century and more ago, sociobiology has been latched onto by people who seek to justify the unjustifiable. Conservatives seize on the principle of natural selection to maintain that everything that exists should be left alone, because it was made that way by the god of adaptation. But this is not so. It ignores genetic drift, whereby characteristics come into being that provide no evolutionary advantage, but also no disadvantage, and so survive despite Darwinian selection, not because of it. The actual essence of the Darwinian principle of selection is not that a trait must be well adapted in order to survive, but that it not be *poorly* adapted relative to other traits. It is possible for some features to continue to develop after they have fulfilled their original evolutionary function. Human intellectual ability is probably an example of this. It grew far beyond what was necessary for human survival in the eons during which it was physically developing (although perhaps not beyond or even up to what is necessary for survival in the nuclear age; indeed it may yet prove to be ultimately maladaptive by destroying the species).

McElvaine's summary of the conservative and liberal positions on human nature is balanced and fair-minded, even though he strongly disagrees with these views. By reporting and engaging opposing arguments, McElvaine makes it more likely that liberals and conservatives will consider his argument: that liberal views on social and gender equality are actually supported by biological evidence about human nature.[12]

5N Lead Your Readers to an Interesting Conclusion

Over the course of your essay, you will develop the significance of your claims. All your analysis should sustain your main argument interestingly. As you lead your readers to their destination, give them plenty of signposts and evidence in the paragraphs. By the time you reach your concluding paragraph, your readers will be ready for you to put your ideas back into a broader context.

There is no formula for a concluding paragraph, just as there is no formula for an introductory or supporting paragraph. Even so, there are certain things historians look for in a conclusion. A conclusion must reflect on the essay and answer the "Who cares?" question once again. A strong conclusion will not simply repeat the introduction. If the essay has truly developed and sustained an idea with interest, then there should be a new way to sum things up. How are the findings of the essay significant? How might the findings of the essay change how the readers think?

One example of a concise but interesting conclusion can be found in Liana Vardi's article "Imagining the Harvest in Early Modern Europe," which addresses the depiction of peasants by early-modern European artists and writers. Over time, representations of peasants had less to do with farm work and more to do with rustic leisure. She concludes:

> The eighteenth century thus adopted a new vision of the peasant. As a laborer, he was harmless and piteous and therefore a natural object of charity and paternalist concern. As an independent farmer, he was virtuous, hardworking, and devoted to his family. Anxious to learn and to be guided, the peasant emerged as a fitting citizen of the state. By the end of the eighteenth century, this figure had become an emblem for mankind.[13]

She summarizes her argument but she goes beyond it, suggesting, in the final sentence, that there was a broader significance to this image of the peasant.

✍ **REVIEW** ✍

1. Be prepared to write several drafts.
2. Explain your purpose clearly.
3. Structure your argument carefully.
4. Define your terms.
5. Deal with counterarguments.
6. Make your conclusion count.

5N

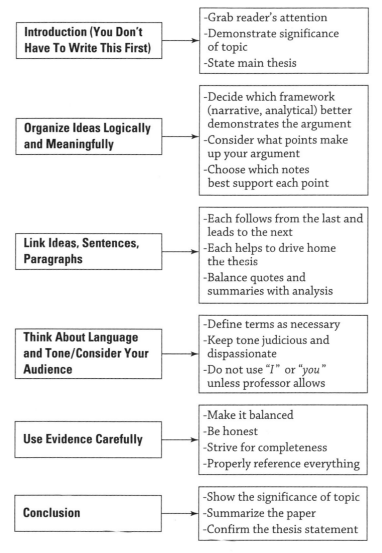

| Introduction (You Don't Have To Write This First) | → | -Grab reader's attention
-Demonstrate significance of topic
-State main thesis |

| Organize Ideas Logically and Meaningfully | → | -Decide which framework (narrative, analytical) better demonstrates the argument
-Consider what points make up your argument
-Choose which notes best support each point |

| Link Ideas, Sentences, Paragraphs | → | -Each follows from the last and leads to the next
-Each helps to drive home the thesis
-Balance quotes and summaries with analysis |

| Think About Language and Tone/Consider Your Audience | → | -Define terms as necessary
-Keep tone judicious and dispassionate
-Do not use "*I*" or "*you*" unless professor allows |

| Use Evidence Carefully | → | -Make it balanced
-Be honest
-Strive for completeness
-Properly reference everything |

| Conclusion | → | -Show the significance of topic
-Summarize the paper
-Confirm the thesis statement |

Flowchart Chapter 5 Writing Your First Draft

6 Narrative Techniques for Historians

You may decide to organize your essay into one long narrative, or you may organize it along analytical lines, using short narratives to illustrate particular points of analysis. The narrative approach is often used in political and intellectual history, while analytical organization is often used in social, cultural, and economic history. Either way, historical writers use narratives.

6A Combine Chronology with Causation

In narratives, historians use time to give structure to the past. For this reason, narratives have some obvious chronological features: a beginning, a middle, and an end. This may seem simple, but in the hands of a skilled historian a narrative's events do not just follow each other; early events cause subsequent events to happen.

If you are crafting a narrative, your first task will be to select influential events and then place them in chronological order. This is vital to understanding the causes of things, and it is not as easy as you may think. For example, historians draw on the accounts of both Muslims and Christians when they write about the Crusades. Unfortunately the two religions kept different calendars, meaning historians must translate the dates of one into the dates of the other to form a coherent chronology. Sometimes you will not know a firm date for an event; you must do your best to place it in relation to another source. Eighteenth-century English parish records tell when children were baptized, but not when they were born. If you wish to establish an individual's date of birth, you will have to find another source that tells you how long families and churches waited before baptizing their children. Placing events in a chronology is more than just an exercise; it helps you understand change over time.

6B Get a Sense of Change and Continuity

Once you have established the sequence of events, you will begin to get a sense of how some things changed over time while other things remained the same. Which events were entirely predictable in the context of the times? Which events were unexpected? This is not as easy as it sounds. Historical actors might have interpreted the same continuities and changes differently from one another. In 1833, the British Parliament emancipated all colonial slaves. Politicians and activists had been debating abolishing the slave trade, ameliorating the lives of slaves, and emancipating them from bondage for more than thirty years. From the perspective of London, some people may have seen emancipation as predictable and perhaps even inevitable. From the perspective of a Barbadian slave, who probably was unable to keep abreast of London politics, emancipation may have come as a sudden and dramatic change in status. But even that interpretation could be too simple. After emancipation, former masters invented numerous ways to coerce former slaves. Sugar production still required land, labor, and capital, all of which remained available to plantation owners and unavailable to former slaves. Former slaves might have felt more continuity than change.[1] In any case, it would be difficult to sort out such problems without establishing a firm chronology.

6C Select the Key Participants in Your Story

If you were telling a narrative of emancipation in Barbados, you might choose to focus on former slaves and masters. You might also work on slave women entrepreneurs, previously freed townsmen, colonial bankers, or government officials. Remember, your story must make an argument. Do certain individuals illustrate the argument of your narrative better than others? Were certain individuals more significant agents of change than others? You may wish to exclude some people from your narrative altogether, or relegate them to the background.

6D Find Your Own Voice as a Narrator

Discovering your own voice as a narrator will be especially challenging the first time you try it. Every historian does this differently, but one rule always applies: every narrator must be as faithful as possible to the people and events of the past.

1. The Omniscient Narrator. Some historians prefer to recede into the background, telling their story from the perspective of an omniscient outsider while refraining from making comments about themselves or their engagement with the source materials. In his account of India's anticolonial rebellion of 1857, *The Great Mutiny*, Christopher Hibbert uses this style of narration. He is arguing that the rebellion began when British officers ordered Indian troops (*sepoys*) to use a new kind of bullet cartridge:

> One day in January 1857 a low-caste labourer at Dum-Dum asked a sepoy for a drink of water from his *lota*. The sepoy, being a Brahmin, had naturally refused: his caste would not allow him to grant such a request; he had just scoured his *lota*; the man would defile it by his touch. "You will soon lose your caste altogether," the labourer told him. "For the Europeans are going to make you bite cartridges soaked in cow and pork fat. And then where will your caste be?"[2]

2. The Uncertain Narrator. Not all historians feel that their sources permit such an omniscient narration. In fact, great controversy surrounds the origins of this 1857 rebellion. Sometimes historians use less-certain strategies of narration to reveal the ambiguities of their source materials. Writers can strengthen a narrative by informing readers of the limits of their interpretations. John Demos uses such a strategy in a book called *The Unredeemed Captive*, which is about Eunice Williams, an English girl who was captured by Mohawks in the Deerfield Massacre of 1704. After her abduction, Eunice adapted to the ways of the Kahnawake Iroquois. This disturbed her family, but it did not stop them from trying to bring her back to Massachusetts. Demos worked with limited sources, mostly the letters and diaries of Eunice's English relatives. The family spent decades trying to learn about Eunice, but in the end they recorded very little information. Demos struggled to extract meaning from these scarce sources, but his narrative is at its most compelling when he speculates about the changes in Eunice's life:

> Different it was, very different. And yet, within a relatively short time, it took. By 1707, Eunice was reported to be "unwilling to return." And the Indians—including, one would presume, her new family—"would as soon part with their hearts" as with this successfully "planted" child.[3]

6E   Choose Your Own Beginning and End

The past is interconnected across chronological and geographical boundaries, but every narrative must have a beginning and an end. You will find it challenging to decide when to start and stop your story. Hibbert begins his story of the 1857 rebellion with a description of a typical working day for Sir Thomas Metcalfe, British representative to the king of Delhi.

6E

> He returned from his office at half past two for dinner at three. After dinner he sat reading for a time before going down to the billiard-room. A game of billiards was followed by two hours spent on the terrace contemplating the river. Then it was time for a light supper and an evening hookah. Immediately the clock struck eight, he stood up and went to bed, undoing his neckcloth and throwing it, together with his well-tailored coat, on to the floor to be picked up by the appropriate servant. If this or any other servant did not perform his duties to the master's entire satisfaction, Sir Thomas would send for a pair of white kid gloves which were presented to him on a silver salver.

These he would draw on with becoming dignity, then firmly pinch the culprit's ear.[4]

Hibbert is not just telling a story about an indolent, autocratic colonial official. Hibbert uses the beginning to set the scene for a larger story about how Indians rebelled against British authority, how British forces crushed the rebels after great loss of life, and how this experience transformed South Asia and the British Empire.

Hibbert sets the opening scene in Delhi because his narrative will reach its climax when the British recapture the city. His narrative ends when the British banish the king of Delhi:

> The trial lasted more than two months; but the verdict was never in doubt. On 29 March he was found guilty on all charges and later sentenced to be transported for life to Rangoon. He left Delhi in October accompanied by Jawan Bakht, another young son whom he had had by a concubine, and by a most unwilling Zinat Mahal who, by now "quite tired of him," described him as "troublesome, nasty, cross old fellow." He died on 7 November 1862 in Rangoon where the descendants of his son, Jawan Bakht, are still living today.[5]

Hibbert concludes his narrative at this point for a number of reasons. The rebellion ended in various ways for many people, but for Hibbert the exile of the king of Delhi represents the end of the rebellion. One of the causes of the rebellion had been a dispute over who would succeed the king. Much of the rebellion had taken place in and around Delhi. The exile of the king draws several strands of the story to a close, while Hibbert mentions the descendants of the king as a way of emphasizing the enduring legacy of the rebellion. Follow Hibbert's example when you conclude a historical narrative: choose a beginning and an ending that suit your story and your argument.

6F Write a Narrative with Well-Chosen Details

Every narrative has some easily recognized components. A narrative has a narrator; it is organized chronologically; it develops a story; and it has main characters, a plot, and a setting. Historical narratives share many features with other forms of storytelling, such as novels and epic poems. One overarching narrative is often supported by shorter narratives and well-chosen details. A story within a story often illustrates the general argument. During the fifth century BCE, a Greek adventurer and storyteller named Herodotus wrote one of the first historical narratives. He used dramatic tension and colorful description to help his readers imagine the past. While recreating the Persian invasion of Greece in 480 BCE, Herodotus described how the emperor Xerxes and his huge army destroyed the small contingent of Spartans guarding the pass at Thermopylae. Herodotus did not simply say that the outnumbered Spartans were brave and fought to the death. Herodotus did not just tell readers that the Spartans were calm when the massive Persian forces came into sight; he told how the Spartans ignored the Persians and combed their hair. Instead of describing every episode of bravery, Herodotus selected the story of one Spartan soldier named Dieneces for special mention:

> It is said before the battle he was told by a native of Trachis that, when the Persians shot their arrows, there were so many of them that they hid the sun. Dieneces, however, quite unmoved by the thought of the strength of the Persian army, merely remarked: "This is pleasant news . . . if the Persians hide the sun, we shall have our battle in the shade."[6]

6G Write a Narrative to Support an Argument

Herodotus was not just telling a story about a gutsy warrior at Thermopylae. He was selecting specific events to illustrate a broader interpretation. Historians use such anecdotes and stories to make arguments, and the best storytellers can wrap a powerful argument within a seamless narrative. When Herodotus presented his work to the Athenian public, he used dramatic techniques to make a connection with his audience: Xerxes lost the war because he had too much pride, the downfall of many a character in Greek drama. Herodotus told the story of Thermopylae because he wanted to show in a colorful way that the Spartans had fought bravely in defense of a united Greece. He also wanted to draw a stark contrast between the Greeks, who died willingly for their liberty, and the Persians, who had to whip their troops to make them fight.[7] The Greeks were clearly superior. Herodotus, like other historians, used a narrative to make an argument. That argument was supported by specific evidence.

❧ REVIEW ❧

1. Use anecdotes to make deliberate points.
2. Include causes and consequences.
3. Control your materials: pick the characters and events you need to make your argument.

Identify a Beginning and End
-How can you narrow your focus?
-What is significant about this time period?

Focus on Specific People
-Who is important to this topic?
-Why are these people important?

Tell What Happens
-What are the significant events?
-Why do these events occur?
-How accurate is the source's perspective?
-Are there holes in your source information?

Evaluate Your Points
-Do the events support an argument?
-Did you analyze the events, or did you just
 summarize what happened?

Flowchart Chapter 6 Representing the Past

7 Writing Sentences in History

Historians share a common goal with all writers: to communicate ideas effectively. Historians differ from other writers on some of the conventions for achieving this goal. This causes some confusion among writers who hail from other disciplines, but even so, no historical convention is arbitrary; all of them help historians represent the past as accurately as possible. While you are writing and revising, use these conventions to your advantage.

7A Choose Verbs That Are Precise

Verbs form the heart of every sentence because they convey the action. Every writer should select precise verbs and avoid vague ones, and this principle is decidedly true for historians.

What is a vague verb? For starters, verbs of being are vague, but as you can see, sometimes it is difficult to avoid them. The order of ideas in the sentence may dictate that you use *is*, *are*, or another form of the verb *to be*. Still, beginning writers tend to overuse verbs of being, a problem that drains the color out of their writing. Why write "Queen Victoria was in power for sixty-four years" when you can write "Queen Victoria reigned for sixty-four years"? If you find yourself writing with a verb of being, look for a noun or an adjective that has a precise verb counterpart.

7B Make Passive Sentences Active

Historians try to avoid the passive voice. One of the purposes of historical writing is to uncover who did what, when. The worst thing a historian can do is to create silence and confusion about the past, which is what the passive voice often does. The passive voice can obliterate historical actors altogether: "America was discovered." By whom? If you cannot write an active sentence like "Columbus discovered America" with any certainty, then you owe your readers an explanation.

As you read more history, you will start to notice that passive sentences often indicate weak reasoning. This is true of history, but it is not necessarily true of other disciplines. Some authors, especially natural scientists, use the passive voice to downplay their personal involvement in research. In fact, one of the biggest challenges for historians of science is to cut through this prose and learn just how scientists did involve themselves in research.

There are circumstances when it is appropriate for historians to use the passive voice. The best writers might include one or two passive sentences on a page. You may wish to put a historical subject at the end of a sentence: "America was discovered by Columbus." The best place for Columbus may be at the end, depending on the order of ideas in the sentence or the paragraph. But even though there are some circumstances when passive verbs are appropriate, passive sentences often confuse the order of ideas. They should be used sparingly (in which sentence I use the passive because I want to emphasize the word *sparingly*).

7C Write in the Past Tense

Unlike writers in other disciplines, historians write almost everything in the past tense. This is not an arbitrary peculiarity. Writing in the past tense helps historians place people and events in an intelligible chronological order.

Historians prefer the past tense, but verb tense is often the subject of some confusion. This is largely because scholars who write about literature have a different set of conventions. A literary critic might

7B

write "In *Black Boy*, Richard Wright speaks eloquently and forcefully against American racism and capitalism." Wright's words ring just as true today as they did in 1937 when he wrote them. For the purposes of writing about literature, the present tense gives an author's ideas a sense of immediacy.

Literary classics have a powerful effect on readers today, but historians want to place Wright's novel within the context of his life and times. Wright does not really speak today; he died in 1960. He wrote *Black Boy* during the Great Depression, when he joined the growing American communist party. At the time readers interpreted Wright's work differently than they do today. Using the present tense confuses the chronology of Wright's life and times, while using the past tense enables writers to arrange one event in relationship to another. Historians usually write in the present tense only when they are discussing recent works or living scholars.

7D Avoid Split Infinitives If You Can

In English, the infinitive is formed by adding the preposition *to*, as in "to be or not to be." Shakespeare could have split the infinitive and written "to bravely be or not to be," but that would have prompted the audience to throw vegetables. Generally speaking, it is a bad idea to place words between *to* and the verb; it throws off the logical order of ideas in the sentence.

Even so, there are circumstances when it is appropriate to split an infinitive. Sometimes it just sounds better. There is a good reason for *Star Trek* beginning with the phrase "to boldly go where no man has gone before." If the infinitive is put back together, listen to the result: "To go boldly where no man has gone before." How uninspiring. In this case, a split infinitive is better than having an adverb in an unnatural location.

7E Put Verbs in Your Sentences

Theoretically, a sentence can be a sentence only if it has a verb. And yet, as you can see from the "How uninspiring" sentence in the previous section, it is possible to use a verbless sentence as an interjection.

There are other uses for them, too. Verbless sentences do add punch and color to writing, but they really do not have a place in formal writing, which is the kind of writing historians usually do. When you write a verbless sentence in a work of history, you are inviting your reader to apply the red ink.

7F Put Your Ideas in an Intelligible Order

You must put your ideas in an order that your audience will understand. This is not as easy as it sounds. After weeks of reading and research on a historical topic, you will be steeped in the complexities of how people, ideas, and events are interrelated. But when you write, you must unravel that complexity and place your ideas in a sequence of words. In each sentence, you must imagine what your audience needs to know first, second, and third.

1. Keep Related Words Together. You may think it makes sense to say "The tail-gunner saw a cloud form over Hiroshima in the shape of a mushroom," because you already know how these ideas are related. Nevertheless, your audience can only get a sense of the relationship of ideas from the way you place the words, and in this case the words are placed poorly. After all, the shape of the mushroom does not relate to Hiroshima; it relates to the cloud. The audience would understand the sentence better if you wrote, "The tail-gunner saw a mushroom-shaped cloud form over Hiroshima." If you keep related words together, you will lead readers seamlessly through your sentence. If you keep unrelated words together, readers will have to pause and sort out the jumble.

2. Keep Pronouns Close to the Words They Represent. By definition, a pronoun substitutes for a noun, but your readers must know which noun. You know in your head which pronoun relates to which noun, but your readers must infer the relationship from the way you place the words, and you must leave them in no doubt.

The best way to avoid misunderstanding is to place the pronoun close to the noun it modifies. Here is a sentence with a confusing pronoun: "Benjamin West's painting of the death of General Wolfe demonstrates his original, American style." Does "his" refer to West or to Wolfe? "His" is closer to "Wolfe," and your readers will probably infer that "his" represents Wolfe, unless, of course, they know the painting. Anyone who has seen this painting knows that Wolfe is dressed in a British uniform and does not appear to be particularly American. The author has to mean that West, not Wolfe, had an American style, but the meaning does not come through in the sentence.

3. Keep Subjects and Verbs Close Together. The principal relationship in a sentence is between the subject and the verb. Do not put too much between them. Take a look at this sentence: "Eleanor Roosevelt, during the presidency of Franklin Roosevelt, wrote a syndicated column." To read this sentence, you must hold "Eleanor Roosevelt" in the back of your mind until you find out what she is doing. The sentence would express the ideas more effectively if it were rewritten like this: "During the presidency of Franklin Roosevelt, Eleanor Roosevelt wrote a syndicated column." Generally speaking, it is acceptable to place a short statement in between a subject and verb, as in "Eleanor Roosevelt, the First Lady, wrote a syndicated column." Just don't put too much between a subject and a verb.

7G Begin a Sentence on Common Ground and Gradually Build a New Point

Writing a sentence is not just about arranging the ideas in an orderly way. In history, as in all writing, a sentence is a place to develop an idea. A well-written sentence gives the reader a sense of direction.

Start by summarizing the previous sentence or by mentioning an idea that you and your reader hold in common; then build toward your original point. A weak pair of sentences would say "General Lee's horse was named Traveler. Fine horses were hard to find in those years, but Traveler was one of the best." The reader has to jump from Traveler to a general statement about horses and then back to Traveler. A better pair of sentences would build from Traveler toward a general statement about horses: "General Lee's horse was named Traveler. He was one of the best horses at a time when good horses were hard to find." The first sentence moves from General Lee to Traveler; then the second sentence moves from Traveler to a general statement about horses. The sentences have a smooth connection.

7H Place the Emphasis at the End

If you are developing your ideas over the course of a sentence, then the end of the sentence should be interesting and emphatic. One master of emphatic writing (and speaking) was Winston Churchill. Here is what he wrote about the Crusades in one of his books, *The Birth of Britain*:

> The Crusading spirit had for some time stirred the minds of men all over western Europe. The Christian kingdoms of Spain had led the way with their holy wars against the Arabs. Now, towards the end of the eleventh century, a new enemy of Christendom appeared fifteen hundred miles to the east. The Seljuk Turks were pressing hard upon the Byzantine Empire in Asia Minor, and harassing devout pilgrims from Europe through Syria to the Holy Land.[1]

Notice how each sentence begins with a connection to the previous sentence. Also notice how each sentence develops in a new direction and concludes with a new idea. The second sentence is especially skillful. It begins by saying something specific about the western European Christians, but then it leads readers to consider the enemies of the Christians, the Arabs.

7I Construct Parallel Forms for Emphasis

One of the best tricks for writing an effective sentence is to learn how to use a parallel construction. This is a kind of repetition in which related ideas are expressed in a rigorously similar grammatical form. For example, on October 8, 1940, as Nazi bombers were pounding Britain, Churchill told the House of Commons that "Death and sorrow will be the companions of our journey; hardship our garment; constancy and valour our only shield. We must be united, we must be undaunted, we must be inflexible."[2] He constructed the first sentence loosely around the repetition of "our," but he constructed the second sentence tightly around the repetition of "we must be." In a parallel construction, a writer expresses parallel ideas by using a parallel grammatical structure.

7J Form the Possessive Correctly

Thus far, this book has not delved into grammar because it is the subject of many other guides to writing. Chances are that if you are now learning how to write history, you have already learned how to write a grammatical sentence. Even so, it is embarrassing to note that many historians, including some well-known professionals, often make one particular grammatical error: they do not know how to form the possessive. Most of the confusion surrounds words that end in the letter *s*.

1. Form the Possessive of a Singular Noun by Adding 's. This is true even when the word ends in the letter *s*. For example, it is correct to write "King Charles's soldiers," or "the duchess's letters."

There are some minor exceptions to this rule. Traditionally, ancient names ending in *s* take only an apostrophe, as in "Moses' laws" or "Jesus' name." However, these constructions are sufficiently awkward that many writers form the possessive with *of*, as in "the laws of Moses" or "the name of Jesus."

2. Form the Possessive of a Plural Noun by Adding an Apostrophe. This is true when the plural is formed by adding an *s*, for example, "the Redcoats' muskets" or "the Wright brothers' airplane."

3. Don't Bother Using an Apostrophe to Form the Plural of Abbreviations and Numbers. It used to be standard practice to use apostrophes to form plurals, for example, "PC's were first manufactured during the 1980's." Many style manuals now consider this use of the apostrophe to be old-fashioned. Omit the apostrophe and just write "PCs" and "the 1980s." Use an apostrophe to form a plural only when there is the possibility of confusion, as in "There are two a's and two i's in assailing."

4. Don't Use an Apostrophe to Form the Plural. It is incorrect to write that "Columbus discovered the America's." Columbus discovered the Americas (at least according to some people).

7K Break the Rules If You Must

You will find that on occasion the conventions just listed will lead you to perform some unnecessary gymnastics. These conventions may even cause you to write an ugly, unnatural sentence. In all such cases, break the rules. Good historical writers understand the spirit of the law as well as the letter. Your first task is to get your meaning across, and to do it persuasively.

∽ **REVIEW** ∾

1. Think! Make every sentence count.
2. Pay special attention to verbs.
3. Use word order to your advantage.

7K

8 Choosing Precise Words

Word choice can make all the difference to a historian, so choose your words precisely. The past abounds with catastrophic examples of poorly chosen words. One such example is the 1840 Treaty of Waitangi, in which the British took New Zealand from the Maoris by mistranslating the word for "sovereignty."[1] This deliberate act of imprecision has caused a century and a half of bad feelings. Chances are that you will never be deliberately imprecise, but you should still choose your words very carefully. Get in the habit of checking your essays for word choice, which is also known as diction. The basic rules of diction often strike inexperienced writers as arbitrary. They are not. The more we read, the more we see that some words are commonly used together and some are not. Common diction ensures common understanding.

8A Be Concise

Some historical writers believe they can demonstrate the complexity of their thoughts by writing sentences that are bursting with unnecessary words. They are wrong. If you make every word count, then you will give your readers the clearest possible picture of your ideas. Why write "It is an undeniable fact that William the Conqueror was instrumental in establishing the Norman regime" when you might easily say "William the Conqueror established the Norman regime"? If you can say something in seven words, why say it in sixteen? Being concise does not mean that all your sentences should be short and choppy; it means that you should not try your readers' patience.

8B Write in Language That Your Audience Can Understand

Most historians write in language that intelligent readers can understand. This standard is subjective, yet it does set history apart from many fields of writing that have developed specialized jargon. Sometimes outside jargon can creep into historical writing. For example, the dictionary defines *hegemony* as dominance, but for professional historians the word is associated with the theoretical writings of an Italian socialist named Antonio Gramsci. You may indeed be writing for an audience that understands hegemony in this precise way, but to a wider audience hegemony may be a jargon word that can cause a misunderstanding.

1. Literary Jargon. History is a form of literature, and historians have learned a great deal from literary critics. Most people who study literature love the English language, but some, in their exuberance, have produced some dreadful writing. People who seem to be different have become the "subjectivized Other." People who like to read good history "valorize the narrativization of the Subject." It may be fun to commit random acts of capitalization, and it is often convenient to stick an "-ize" on a noun to create a verb, but if you are writing for more than just a few literary critics, write in a language that your audience can understand.

2. Social-Science Jargon. History is also one of the social sciences, and history overlaps, in many ways, with the disciplines of anthropology, economics, political science, and sociology. Some social scientists write well, but many prefer tortured jargon to ordinary words. Talking is "interpersonal communication," and a different way of looking at something puts it on "another axis of differentiation." This language is fine for communicating with other social scientists, but really, when is the last time you freely chose to read a book by people who write like this? Social-science jargon will limit the size of your audience.

3. Legal Jargon. Many historians study the law, and some historians even practice the law. Nevertheless, there are important differences between legal writing and historical writing. When lawyers compose legal documents, they are writing for a different audience: the court. They go to great lengths to ensure that their clients will not get into trouble. To avoid trouble, lawyers use archaisms, repetition, and formal words such as "the said," "party to the first part," and "stipulate." This language is not pretty, and it should be used only by lawyers, for lawyers, unless stipulated to by both the party of the first part, who is hereby named the historian, and the party of the second part, which is hereby named the historian's audience. Otherwise, keep legal jargon out of historical writing.

4. Government Jargon. "Officialese," as it is called, is a close cousin of legal jargon. They both have the same purpose: to cover the writer's hindquarters. At least lawyers have the excuse of having to protect their clients; bureaucrats, officers, and politicians use jargon mainly to protect themselves. Either they want to make themselves seem important or they are trying to avoid precise commitments. In his famous essay "Politics and the English Language," George Orwell translated a passage from the Bible—

> I returned and saw under the sun, that the race is not to the swift, nor the battle to the strong, neither yet bread to the wise, nor yet riches to men of understanding, nor yet favor to men of skill; but time and chance happeneth to them all.

into the obscure, pompous language of government:

> Objective consideration of contemporary phenomena compels the conclusion that success or failure in competitive activities exhibits no tendency to be commensurate with innate capacity, but that a considerable element of the unpredictable must invariably be taken into account.[2]

Orwell's point is clear: jargon writers are in the habit of taking concrete examples and beautiful rhythm and turning them into abstract language and meaningless words. Always use precise language that your audience understands.

8C Avoid Pretentious Language

Don't think that you will look smart just by using complicated words. You may only wind up confusing your readers. You may think that central planning had a "procrustean" effect on Soviet engineering, but if your audience does not know that the word means a ruthless disregard for special circumstances, you have not gained much ground with them. Even if they do know what the word means, it may stand out from the overall tone of your argument. Control any urges to use puffed-up vocabulary.

8D Avoid Colloquial Language

Most history instructors expect that you will write in formal English. This means you should avoid slang, contractions, and an overly casual tone. Such informal language, also known as colloquial language, may be inserted as part of a quotation, and you may also use colloquial language outside of formal, academic writing. This book, for example, has a less formal tone than most works of history. Even so, most historians consider colloquial language to be, like, uncool.

8E Be Sensitive to the Politics of Diction

Historical writing has always reflected the politics of the times. Today historians are demonstrating their awareness of discrimination by avoiding intolerant language. Conservatives complain that liberals are forcing a "politically correct" form of "linguistic engineering" on them. Some liberals think that conservatives have not gone far enough to purge the language of offensive usage. The debate will never be resolved, but everyone can agree that writers must meet their audience. Historical writers must keep their eyes and ears open to learn what their audience thinks is appropriate. Some racial designations have changed considerably over the years: "Negro" and "colored" changed to "black" and then "black" started to become "African American." Most historians recognize that all traditions are invented, including linguistic traditions, and they also recognize that people ought to be allowed to come up with a name for themselves.

8F Be Sensitive to Gender-Specific Language

Oscar Wilde said, "Anybody can make history. Only a great man can write it." He said this in the 1890s, and his main point was to call attention to the difference between historical actors and the people who write about them. When historians read this statement today, Wilde's underlying sexist assumptions are readily apparent, even if Wilde might be forgiven for being a creature of his times.

In recent years historians have become more sensitive to gender. This is reflected not only in their intellectual interests but also in their historical writing. Years ago it was acceptable to say, "The historian must analyze sources. He must understand the relevant documents." The masculine pronoun with an antecedent of indeterminate gender was conventional. Fortunately, today there are plenty of female historians, a fact that contradicts the practice of associating nouns like "the historian" with masculine pronouns. Such a construction now seems inaccurate and biased.

To avoid such sexist pitfalls, you may be tempted to change Wilde's second sentence with some keyboard gymnastics: "He/she must understand the relevant documents," or, even worse, you might write "s/he." Add an "http://" and you will have created a new Internet address. Slashed pronouns can usually be prevented by employing simple solutions. First, consider using neutral pronouns like "everyone," "anybody," and "everybody." If that doesn't work, try to change Wilde's sentences from singular to plural: "Historians must analyze sources. They must understand the relevant documents." Changing a gender-specific singular to a gender-neutral plural conveys the same idea without any sexist overtones.

You might also be tempted to substitute the third-person-singular neutral pronoun, "one," for a gender-biased "he." "When one is a historian, one must analyze sources." Occasionally such a construction is appropriate, but most of the time it sounds pretentious.

8G Avoid Euphemisms

Sometimes politically correct language works well, but other times it seems silly. Some linguistic engineering may be necessary to overcome odious rhetorical practices, but nobody is really calling stupid people "intellectually challenged." This is a euphemism, a polite, meaningless word that covers up a harsh reality. The twentieth century seems to have been especially rich in euphemisms: torched villages were "pacified," totalitarian regimes were "people's republics," and used cars were "pre-owned vehicles." Spare your readers the bull.

8H Choose Figurative Language Carefully

When historians write about subjects that are unfamiliar to their readers, it often helps to make an imaginative comparison with something the reader knows. These comparisons often take the form of metaphors and similes. It would be perfectly acceptable to write that "Simón Bolívar participated in the overthrow of Spanish rule in the Americas." It would be more engaging to write, "Simón Bolívar played a role in the overthrow of Spanish rule in the Americas," because this would draw a comparison to the theater. It would be even more colorful to say that "Simón Bolívar was the George Washington of Spanish America," but you might have to sustain the metaphor by comparing evidence about the two leaders. Metaphors and similes add color to historical writing, but it takes practice to use them well.

8I Use Metaphors and Similes Judiciously

There are a number of ways for a metaphor to go awry. You could write that "Simón Bolívar was the John Chilembwe of Spanish America," but this metaphor presents a number of problems. Chances are that people reading an essay on Venezuelan history have never heard of John Chilembwe. This is unfortunate, because in 1915 Chilembwe led a major rebellion against British colonial rule in Nyasaland. Still, the metaphor does not work in a number of other ways. Chilembwe's rebellion failed, whereas Bolívar's succeeded. The comparison is also awkward because it is anachronistic: Chilembwe's revolt happened a century after Bolívar's. It is a good idea to use vivid metaphors and similes, but they must ring true to your audience's ears.

8J Use Color, But Avoid Clichés

Your readers will welcome colorful language, but they will find your colors boring if they are entirely predictable. Colorful expressions that have been overused are called clichés. Replace them with plain language or less predictable metaphors.

Use this simple test to spot a cliché. You are using a cliché if you can remove the last word from the phrase and your readers can automatically fill it in:

- "Queen Elizabeth did not suffer fools . . . (gladly)."
- "Albert Einstein burned the midnight . . . (oil)."
- "The bubonic plague reared its ugly . . . (head)."

8K Use Foreign Words That Are Familiar to Your Audience

Historians often use foreign words in their writing. Some foreign terms have come into common English usage, as in "Nehru was a politician *par excellence*," or "The U.S. Constitution prohibits the *ex post facto* application of laws." However, when you write about the history of a foreign country you may sometimes find yourself in a quandary over how to use foreign terms.

The basic rule of thumb is to use terms that your audience understands. Imagine that you are writing about the history of the amaXhosa, an important group of people who live in South Africa. If you were taking a seminar on southern African history, and you were writing for an instructor who was a specialist in the field, it might be appropriate for you to spell out the name "amaXhosa." This is because specialists in southern African history know that this group of people forms the plural of their collective name by adding the prefix "ama." If you were writing for a more general audience, say, in a survey of world history, you would probably not want to bother teaching your readers about the intricacies of southern African prefixes. In this situation, it is probably best to call your subjects "the Xhosa," a compromise that shows your reader that you are savvy enough not to add English plurals to foreign words. If you were writing for an even broader audience, perhaps in a journalistic piece for an American newspaper, you might want to skip the linguistic complexities altogether and just say "the Xhosas." Above all, it is important to know your audience's capabilities and to meet them on common ground.

8L Check for These Common Diction Problems

It is easy to misuse words and expressions, partly because they are so often misused. Word-processing programs make it possible to search for any given word. If you suspect that you have misused any of the words listed next, run a search on your computer.

If you need further assistance on points of usage, ask a reference librarian to help you find *The New Fowler's Modern English Usage*, ed. R. W. Burchfield (Oxford UK: Oxford University Press, 1996). It is the updated version of H. W. Fowler's classic work on English usage, which is the basis for the following list of common problems that appear in historical writing. The "pocket" version of Fowler may be found at the Oxford Reference online, http://www.oxfordreference .com. The website also contains another very good resource on the use of words, Bryan Garner's *The Oxford Dictionary of American Usage and Style* (New York: Oxford University Press, 2000).

AD and **BC** mean *Anno domini* [the year of our Lord] and Before Christ, respectively. These abbreviations seem to be slipping out of use, in favor of CE and BCE, which mean Common Era and Before Common Era. This new dating system is helpful in world history courses in which diverse approaches to religion are considered. When you think about it, though, the Christian dates are still retained.

All right is proper for formal writing. Many people spell it as "alright," but most authorities regard "alright" as overly casual. It may have been all right for Elvis to sing "That's alright, Mama," but it's not all right to write "alright" in a formal essay.

And/or appears frequently in insecure writing, possibly because it has a legalistic sound to it. "And/or" is not incorrect, but it is inelegant. It implies that the two items that are joined together can be taken apart, which is a fundamentally odd concept. As Burchfield says, it is usually a good idea to avoid it by writing "X or Y or both," or just by writing "or."

Ante- and **anti-** are two Latin prefixes that students often confuse. Ante means "before," whereas *anti* means "against." For example, "antebellum America" refers to America before the Civil War, whereas "antiwar protestors" opposed the war.

Because is a word commonly used in historical writing because historians usually want to learn what caused things to happen. "Harriet Beecher Stowe wrote *Uncle Tom's Cabin* because she was disturbed by slavery." Elementary school English teachers tell students not to start a sentence with "because," and generally speaking they are right. "Because" introduces a clause that depends on another clause; if you reverse the sentence about Harriet Beecher Stowe and start it with the "because" clause you will make it hard for readers to follow the sentence. You need to know what is being caused before you learn why it is being caused. Still, there are circumstances when historical writers make reasonable exceptions to this rule.

Cannot is usually written as one word, not as "can not." Furthermore, "can't" is usually too colloquial for academic writing.

Different is the subject of some debate. Real sticklers will tell you that "different" can only be followed by "from" and not by "than" or "to." The editors of the *Oxford English Dictionary* disagree. They say that people have been using "different to" since 1526 and "different than" since 1644. Is it possible that so many people could be so wrong for so long? "Different from" works best in most cases, especially in formal writing. It is worth noting that "different" can be used unnecessarily, too: "During the Second Triumvirate, Rome had three different leaders." Remove "different" and the sentence means the same thing.

Double negatives are not uncommon in historical writing, but they should be used sparingly. Two negatives always cancel each other out: "Napoleon was not undefeated at Waterloo" is a stupid way to say "Napoleon was defeated at Waterloo." Most of the time you would do well to convert a double negative into a positive. Sometimes double negatives can be used to add irony, as in the first sentence just shown in this entry.

Due to is a bullet worth dodging. You may think that this compound preposition is harmless enough, but generations of history professors have told students not to overuse it. According to Strunk and White, "due to" should be used only to mean "attributable to," as in "Custer's defeat was due to poor intelligence." It should not substitute for "because" or "through," as in "Custer lost the battle due to poor intelligence." Even so, both the proper and improper uses of "due to" are pretty vague. How can Custer's defeat be attributed to poor intelligence? It is impossible to know, even from the proper use of "due to." It might be best to avoid "due to" altogether.

It's and **its** get confused frequently, even though they mean two completely different things. *It's* is the contraction of "it is": "It's not too late to learn how to write history." *Its* is the possessive form of "it": "When Castro lit a Montecristo, its pungent smoke filled the air." If you confuse *it's* and *its*, the only way to salvage your reputation is to tell your reader that it's a typo. It is also worth mentioning that *its'* is not a word in the English language.

Led to. It may be true that "the First World War *led* to the Second World War"; just don't confuse chronology with causation. It is true that 1939 follows 1914, but your readers will expect you to explain how the first war helped to cause the second war. Saying "led to" is often vague.

Lifestyle is an imprecise word that has no place in historical writing. This sentence comes from a student historian's essay: "The lifestyle of the African-American slaves cannot be compared with the lifestyle of the concentration camp inmates." The writer would have done better to discuss their ways of life, their cultures, or their experiences.

Native is a dangerous word to bandy about in historical writing. One might plausibly talk about the native Tahitians just as one might talk about the native French. But don't call the Tahitians "the natives" because you wouldn't call the French "the natives," except perhaps in jest. "The natives" is a term that Europeans once reserved for people from other parts of the world whom they deemed to be uncivilized. Today it is bad form to use this kind of derogatory language. Of course, every rule has its exceptions: the American Indians who live in the United States now prefer to be called the Native Americans.

Novel is sometimes used by beginning students to refer to any large book, even works of history. This is incorrect. By definition, a novel is a work of fiction. A novel cannot be a history.

Regard is misused frequently in compound prepositions like "with regards to" and "in regards to." The prime offenders are bureaucrats, but historical writers misuse "regard," too. There are two proper ways to use *regard*. If it is part of a compound preposition, use the singular "regard," as in "with regard to" or "in regard to." If it is a verb, conjugate accordingly: "as it regards" or "as they regard."

That and **which** have become the subject of considerable confusion among historians and other writers. In these two sentences, which one would you use to connect one clause to another?

1. "Despite the tense atmosphere *that/which* prevailed during the trial, Mandela spoke his mind to the court."
2. "In 1846, the Corn Laws, *that/which* had protected English farmers from foreign competition, were repealed."

Fowler and Burchfield have tried to standardize the use of *that* and *which*. They recommend that authors use *that* in restrictive clauses and *which* in nonrestrictive clauses. What do these grammatical terms mean?

The first example sentence is a restrictive clause. In other words, the information "prevailed during the trial" is essential to the statement "Despite the tense atmosphere." According to Fowler and Burchfield, the first sentence, and all restrictive clauses, should employ *that*.

The second sentence is different because it contains a nonrestrictive clause: "had protected English farmers from foreign competition." This is a parenthetical statement that might just as well be placed in another sentence. If you want to use it in this sentence, use *which*. Fowler and Burchfield recommend using *which* in all other nonrestrictive clauses, too.

If you apply Fowler and Burchfield's rule to your writing, you will attain a higher degree of clarity. Their rule does work well. Unfortunately, even Fowler and Burchfield admit they are fighting an uphill battle for the proper use of *that* and *which*. When you read other historical writers, apply the rule for *that* and *which* and you will notice that there is confusion. To add to the confusion, British writers tend to use *that* and *which* interchangeably.

Tribe is subject to the same rules that govern "native." A long time ago anthropologists defined *tribe* precisely, to mean a group of people who trace their ancestry to one person, real or imagined. Unfortunately, many historians and journalists use it loosely and offensively, to mean any group of people with brown skin. One might talk about "tribal conflict" in Rwanda but not "tribal conflict" in Bosnia. This use of the word *tribe* derives from efforts of European administrators to classify and regulate groups of people in their former colonies. Ironically, some Africans and Native Americans took up the practice and now call themselves "tribes."

✎ REVIEW ✎

1. Choose your words carefully.
2. Spelling counts!
3. Avoid slang and contractions.
4. Be direct—say what you mean.

8L

9 Revising and Editing

This guide is not a cookbook for historians. There is no recipe for writing history, and if you follow the conventions set out in this book there is no guarantee that your writing will become perfect. There is no such thing as a perfect history, and there is no such thing as a "cookbook historian."

Historians understand the conventions for writing history, but all historians have their own ways of writing. Approaches to writing depend partly on personal style and partly on the subject that is being written about. The more you write history, the more you will gain a sense of your own style and interests. And while you are learning about these things, you will also come to know your own strengths and weaknesses. You have probably heard of the ancient Greek inscription over the temple at Delphi: "Know thyself." Get to know your own weaknesses as a writer; then watch out for them.

9A Get Some Perspective on Your Draft

It is important to get some distance from your paper. You must write for an audience, and to do that you must be able to see your writing as someone else sees it. Spend a few days working on other things; putting some distance between yourself and your writing will help you make revisions.

When historians are in the thick of writing, they often have to take a break before they can stand back and assess their own text with any objectivity. If you are lucky, you might have an instructor or friend who is willing to read a first draft and comment on it. In any case, write the best possible draft, and take your critic's comments seriously. Eventually, you will have to share your writing with an audience that is unfamiliar with all your sources and their unique problems. Early comments on a draft can help you assess whether you have made a persuasive case to your audience.

9B Work with a Peer Editor

Find a classmate who can exchange drafts with you. Read each other's drafts and write comments that address these issues in one or two thoughtful sentences.

1. Does the essay make a good impression in terms of grammar, style, and spelling? Just note overall problems in these categories. Proofreading is the responsibility of the author.

2. What historical conflict does this essay solve?

3. In what ways is this historical conflict significant?

4. Suggest one improvement to how the author approaches a historical conflict.

5. Summarize the author's main argument in your own words.

6. Suggest one way for the author to improve his or her argument.

7. Describe the two pieces of evidence that best support the argument. Why are these items the best pieces of evidence?

8. Describe your two favorite inferences.

9. Suggest at least two ways in which the author could improve the use of evidence.

10. Identify two or three paragraph transitions that could be improved and suggest ways to improve them.

11. Describe the conclusion. How could it be made more effective?

9C Revise Your Draft

A critical reader will assess both the strengths and weaknesses of your paper. Sometimes it is difficult to take criticism, but remember that your best critics spend a great deal of time thinking about your work. This in itself is a compliment. Even if you conclude that the critic's advice is bad, the criticism has had the positive effect of making you reconfirm your position.

Now that you have some perspective on your writing, it is time to revise. First address your critic's comments, which may concern both the style and the substance of the paper. Write another draft that incorporates the suggested changes. Then stand back from your paper and assess it again. Have you addressed your critic's comments fully?

No critic, no matter how generous, will tell you everything you need to know to turn your draft into a prize-winning piece of writing. You yourself must take responsibility for revising. One basic strategy of revising is to begin to work on broad revisions to the arguments and narratives, and then work on smaller problems, such as sentences and diction. Finally, you will need to proofread for spelling, grammar, punctuation, and formatting.

9D Evaluate Your Own Arguments and Narratives

A previous section of this book outlined the key components of historical argumentation. Check your writing thoroughly for several things: Does the evidence support the inferences? Are all the inferences fully warranted? Does the argument flow and develop consistently? Will readers find this to be an interesting and significant argument?

Chapter 6 of this book outlined the key components of historical narratives. Check your writing to make sure your audience knows what they need to know in the correct order. Are characters introduced properly? Will your readers find that the chronological sequences of events are in order? Have you included extraneous information that does not drive any of the main stories? Have you established a consistent voice as a narrator?

9E Evaluate Your Sentences and Word Choices

This book has already given some advice on how to write sentences and how to choose words. While you are revising, you must stand back and look at your sentences as your audience would. Have you chosen strong verbs? Is the order of ideas correct? Do sentences start on common ground and develop a new idea?

Also look at your word choices, or diction, as your audience would. Are you writing in a precise language that your audience will understand? Are you writing in language that will distract them from your ideas? Authors of narratives and authors of analytical essays must now make a final check of an important item: Does every component of the essay support the main argument? If not, parts of the essay need to be better integrated, or cut.

9F Proofread the Final Draft

Proofreading is an essential part of writing history. If you sprinkle your writing with minor mistakes, even your most brilliant work will look like a comedy of errors.

Proofreading takes time and patience. Chances are that when you start to proofread, you will already have revised your paper so many times that your eyes will start to wander. Be disciplined. Print your paper, because it is easier to spot mistakes on paper than on the screen. Force yourself to read every word and every line. If this gets too boring, put the writing aside for a short time and come back to it later. You might even try reading the pages in reverse order, so that you focus less on the argument and narrative and more on the proofreading. There is no real way to make proofreading interesting, but still it must be done.

1. Proofread for Punctuation. Sentences often derive a significant part of their meaning from punctuation, which an anecdote will demonstrate. During a heated debate in Britain's House of Lords, one member insulted another. The insulted lord demanded an apology, and the offending lord replied: "I called the Right Honourable Lord a liar it is true and I am sorry for it. And the Right Honourable Lord may punctuate as he pleases."[1]

Imprecise punctuation can indeed cause problems, and these problems are probably more common than you think. You may make mistakes yourself, and you may even notice mistakes in the works of

9F

129

published historians. If you have trouble with punctuation, refer to Turabian or the *Chicago Manual of Style* for guidance. There are plenty of other writing manuals that discuss punctuation, too.

2. Proofread for Spelling. Spelling errors can be the most embarassing of all mistakes. (Or was that embarrassing?) Everybody should use the spell-checking feature on his or her word-processing program. Just remember that it will not catch all spelling mistakes, especially those involving homonyms. After running the spell-checker, you should print and recheck the paper yourself.

3. Check Your Formatting. Make sure you have used a consistent word-processing format throughout the paper. A consistent format is crucial because aberrations are distracting. Your readers will also expect a simple format. Typically, history professors prefer 12-point Times font with one-inch margins and lines double-spaced. Be sure that the pages are numbered, and that your name and the paper's title are on the first page. (Some professors may ask for a title page. This is a tradition that is a waste of paper, in this author's opinion.) While you are checking your format, be sure to print out the paper and check things that do not necessarily appear on the screen when you are writing, such as footnotes, margins, and page numbers.

4. Read Your Paper Aloud. Reading aloud is the oldest trick for catching writing problems, and it should be the last thing you do before you submit your work. Reading aloud forces you to review every word. Others may think you are eccentric, but your readers will appreciate the end result: a better piece of writing.

9G Keep the Rules in Mind, But Enjoy Your Writing

Writing history can be difficult, but most historical writers consider themselves to be quite privileged. Research and writing can be both exhilarating and plodding; the end result is almost always worth the effort.

~∞ **REVIEW** ∞~

1. Take a break to give yourself some perspective.
2. Choose a meaningful title.
3. Ask someone else to read your paper and comment on it.
4. Revise, revise, revise—everything from arguments to spelling and punctuation.
5. Check and re-check.
6. Keep all notes and drafts.
7. Make a copy and save it.

Assess Your Draft(s)
-Evidence sufficient?
-Inferences valid?
-References accurate and complete?
-Argument consistent and logically organized?
-Terms clearly defined?

↓

Proofread Your Draft
-Sentences well-ordered, well-phrased, and clear?
-Words precisely used?
-Punctuation, grammar, and spelling correct?
-Formatting, font, and font size acceptable?

↓

Check Your Citations
-Bibliography up to date?
-Footnotes/endnotes complete and accurate?

Flowchart Chapter 9 Writing Your Final Draft

9G

NOTES

Introduction

1. Peter Novick, *That Noble Dream: The "Objectivity Question" and the American Historical Profession* (Cambridge, UK: Cambridge University Press, 1988), 7.

2. Thucydides, *The Peloponnesian War*, trans. Rex Warner (New York: Penguin Books, 1954; repr. 1984), 145.

3. J. R. McNeill, *Something New under the Sun: An Environmental History of the Twentieth-Century World* (New York: Norton, 2000).

4. Alfred W. Crosby, *The Columbian Exchange: Biological and Cultural Consequences of 1492* (Westport, CT: Greenwood Press, 1972).

Chapter 1

1. Bruce Mazlish, "The Art of Reviewing," *Perspectives* 39, no. 2 (February 2001). American Historical Association, http://www.historians.org/perspectives/issues/2001/0102/. Accessed March 1, 2011.

Chapter 2

1. For an introduction to the role of the scientific method in the professionalization of history during the nineteenth century, see Joyce Appleby, Lynn Hunt, and Margaret Jacob, *Telling the Truth about History* (New York: W.W. Norton & Co., 1994).

2. For a broader discussion of these research questions, see Richard Marius, *A Short Guide to Writing about History*, 2nd ed. (New York: HarperCollins, 1995), 33–43.

3. Michel-Rolph Trouillot, *Silencing the Past: Power and the Production of History* (Boston: Beacon Press, 1995), 49–53.

4. Loren R. Graham, *The Ghost of the Executed Engineer: Technology and the Fall of the Soviet Union* (Cambridge, MA: Harvard University Press, 1993).

5. Jorge Luis Borges, *Ficciones*, trans. Emecé Editores (New York: Grove Press, 1962), 112.

Chapter 3

1. Cicero, *Pro Publio Sestio*, 2.62. As quoted by John Bartlett and Justin Kaplan, eds., *Bartlett's Familiar Quotations*, 16th ed. (Boston: Little Brown, 1992), 87.

2. These suggestions are taken from Gordon Harvey, *Writing with Sources* (Cambridge, MA: Harvard University, 1995), 27–29.

3. Joyce Lee Malcolm, *To Keep and Bear Arms: The Origins of an Anglo-American Right* (Cambridge, MA: Harvard University Press, 1994), 143.

4. Jack P. Greene, *Pursuits of Happiness: The Social Development of Early Modern British Colonies and the Formation of American Culture* (Chapel Hill: University of North Carolina Press, 1988), 61.

5. E. P. Thompson, *The Making of the English Working Class* (New York: Vintage Books, 1963; pbk. ed. 1966), 193–94.

6. Walter MacDougall, *The Heavens and the Earth: A Political History of the Space Age* (New York: Basic Books, 1985), 8.

7. MacDougall, *Heavens and Earth*, 8.

8. Harvey, *Writing with Sources*, 21–23.

9. Thomas C. Holt, *The Problem of Freedom: Race, Labor, and Politics in Jamaica, 1832–1938* (Baltimore: Johns Hopkins University Press, 1992), 83.

10. Harvey, *Writing with Sources*, 13–16.

Chapter 4

1. Walt Whitman, "The Real War Will Never Get in the Books," in *Specimen Days* (New York: Signet Classic, 1961), 112.

2. Deborah E. Lipstadt, *Denying the Holocaust* (New York: Penguin, 1993).

3. Philip D. Curtin, *The Atlantic Slave Trade: A Census* (Madison: University of Wisconsin Press, 1969).

4. Prasenjit Duara, *Culture, Power, and the State: Rural North China, 1900–1942* (Stanford, CA: Stanford University Press, 1988). Philip C. C. Huang, *The Peasant Economy and Social Change in North China* (Stanford, CA:

Stanford University Press, 1985). Ramon Myers, *The Chinese Peasant Economy: Agricultural Development in Hopei and Shantung, 1840–1940* (Cambridge, MA: Harvard University Press, 1970).

5. Gerald L. Geison, *The Private Science of Louis Pasteur* (Princeton, NJ: Princeton University Press, 1995), 149–56.

6. James Fairhead and Melissa Leach, *Misreading the African Landscape: Society and Ecology in a Forest-Savanna Mosaic* (Cambridge, UK: Cambridge University Press, 1996).

7. Jan Vansina, *Living with Africa* (Madison: University of Wisconsin Press, 1994), 16–17.

8. Pete Daniel, *Standing at the Crossroads: Southern Life in the Twentieth Century* (Baltimore: Johns Hopkins University Press, 1986; 2nd ed. 1996), 21–22.

9. James C. Cobb, *The Most Southern Place on Earth: The Mississippi Delta and the Roots of Regional Identity* (New York: Oxford University Press, 1992), 290.

10. Margaret Washington Creel, "Gullah Attitudes Toward Life and Death," and Robert Farris Thompson, "Kongo Influences on African-American Artistic Culture," in *Africanisms in American Culture*, ed. Joseph E. Holloway (Bloomington: Indiana University Press, 1990), 81–82, 154.

11. John Janzen and Wyatt MacGaffey, *An Anthology of Kongo Religion: Primary Texts from Lower Zaïre* (Lawrence: University of Kansas, 1974), 73–75.

12. Jules David Prown, "Mind in Matter: An Introduction to Material Culture Theory and Method," in *Material Life in America, 1600–1860*, ed. Robert Blair St. George (Boston: Northeastern University Press, 1991), 17–35. Thanks to Elizabeth Abrams for suggesting this article.

13. Charles S. Maier, *The Unmasterable Past: History, Holocaust, and German National Identity* (Cambridge, MA: Harvard University Press, 1988), 1.

14. Georges Lefebvre, *The Coming of the French Revolution*, trans. R. R. Palmer (Princeton, NJ: Princeton University Press, 1947; rev. ed. 1989).

15. Betty Jo Teeter Dobbs, *The Janus Face of Genius: The Role of Alchemy in Newton's Thought* (Cambridge, UK: Cambridge University Press, 1991).

Chapter 5

1. Samuel Eliot Morison, "History as a Literary Art: An Appeal to Young Historians," *Old South Leaflets* ser. 2, no. 1 (Boston: Old South Association, 1946): 7.

2. Caroline Walker Bynum, *Holy Feast and Holy Fast: The Religious Significance of Food to Medieval Women* (Berkeley and Los Angeles: University of California Press, 1987), 1.

3. Samuel K. Cohn, Jr., "The Black Death: End of a Paradigm," *American Historical Review* 107, no. 3 (June 2002): 703. Cohn's citations have not been included in this quotation.

4. Paul Josephson, "The Ocean's Hot Dog: The Development of the Fish Stick," *Technology and Culture* 49, no. 1 (January 2008): 41.

5. W. Jeffrey Bolster, "Putting the Ocean in Atlantic History: Maritime Communities and Marine Ecology in the Northwest Atlantic, 1500–1800," *American Historical Review* 113, no. 1 (February 2008): 19–47, references to pp. 19–23.

6. Daniel Headrick, *The Tools of Empire: Technology and European Imperialism in the Nineteenth Century* (Oxford, UK: Oxford University Press, 1981), 85–86.

7. A. I. Sabra, "Situating Arabic Science: Locality Versus Essence," History of Science Society Distinguished Lecture, published in *Isis* 87, no. 4 (December 1996): 654–70. Quotation from p. 668.

8. William Cronon, *Changes in the Land: Indians, Colonists, and the Ecology of New England* (New York: Hill and Wang, 1983), 6.

9. Carl Degler, *In Search of Human Nature: The Decline and Revival of Darwinism in American Social Thought* (Oxford, UK: Oxford University Press, 1991), vii.

10. Robert Jay Lifton, *The Nazi Doctors: Killing and the Psychology of Genocide* (New York: Basic Books, 1986), 341, 378.

11. William Sheridan Allen, *The Nazi Seizure of Power: The Experience of a Single German Town, 1922–1945* (New York: Franklin Watts, 1965; rev. ed. 1984), 207.

12. Robert S. McElvaine, *Eve's Seed: Biology, the Sexes, and the Course of History* (New York: McGraw-Hill, 2001), 26–32.

13. Liana Vardi, "Imagining the Harvest in Early Modern Europe," *The American Historical Review* 101, no.5 (December 1996): 1397.

Chapter 6

1. Franklin W. Knight, *The Caribbean: The Genesis of a Fragmented Nationalism*, 2nd ed. (New York: Oxford University Press, 1990).

2. Christopher Hibbert, *The Great Mutiny: India 1857* (New York: Penguin Books, 1978), 63.

3. John Demos, *The Unredeemed Captive: A Family Story from Early America* (New York: Vintage Books, 1994), 146.

4. Hibbert, *Great Mutiny*, 24.

5. Hibbert, *Great Mutiny*, 388.

6. Herodotus, *The Histories*, trans. Aubrey de Sélincourt (New York: Penguin Classics, 1954; rev. ed. 1983), 519.

7. Chester W. Starr, *A History of the Ancient World*, 4th ed. (New York: Oxford University Press, 1991), 294–95.

Chapter 7

1. Winston S. Churchill, *The Birth of Britain*, vol. 1 in *History of the English Speaking Peoples* (New York: Dodd, Mead, 1956; Bantam, 1974), 131.

2. *Bartlett's Familiar Quotations*, 16th ed., p. 620.

Chapter 8

1. James Belich, *The Victorian Interpretation of Racial Conflict: The Maori, the British, and the New Zealand Wars* (Montreal and Kingston: McGill and Queen's University Press, 1989), 20–21.

2. George Orwell, "Politics and the English Language," in *Fields of Writing*, eds. Nancy Comley et al., 4th ed. (New York: St. Martin's Press, 1994), 618.

Chapter 9

1. Mary Refling et al., "British Wit in the House of Lords," H-Albion bulletin board, July 8–10, 1997, http://networks.h-net.org/h-albion. Accessed January 20, 2015.